Didier Lehénaff

The Experts' Guide to the Triathlon

SPORTSBOOKS

The Experts' Guide to the Triathlon
is the first title in the series 'Practical Sports'
from SportsBooks.

SportsBooks Limited
PO Box 422
Cheltenham
GL50 2YN
United Kingdom
Tel: 08700 713 965
Fax: 08700 750 888
e-mail   randall@sportsbooks.ltd.uk
Website   www.sportsbooks.ltd.uk

ISBN 1-899807-14-4
© Éditions Chiron, 2001 – 25, rue Monge, 75005 PARIS.
Printed by Biddles Ltd.

This work is dedicated to Karen Smyers and Greg Welch, two of the greatest triathletes our sport has known. They won all the sport's biggest prizes but one, the opportunity to take part in the Olympic Games. It was a dream ruined by illness just months before the 2000 Sydney Games.

In recollection of what were "Les Trois Sports" (The Three Sports), my thoughts go also to René Tasqué, an unknown triathlete from the interwar period and a solitary witness still alive to the previous history of the triathlon. Thanks also to Béatrice, Isabelle, Karen, Susanne, Brett, Eduardo, Grégoire, Laurent, Lothar, Luc, Philippe and Simon, who illuminate this work. I thought I knew a lot about the triathlon, but the more I listened to them the more I discovered the extent of my ignorance.

Forgiveness to those who would have also deserved to be a part of this snapshot of the triathlon family, triathletes and highly skilled coaches (forgiveness Claude, Olivier, Patrick, Philippe and Rob), forgiveness to all those who illuminated our weekends for more than 15 years.

Thank you finally and infinitely to Dany, Caroline and Kévin, for their support.

CONTENTS

FOREWORD

The idea for this book came to me when I was reviewing literature in preparation for a triathlon conference some years ago. I had been delving into my bibliographical references in various books and magazines which could be classified generally into three distinct categories.

- The monthly magazines, more or less specialised (triathlon, multisports, countryside, etc.) where the contents always vary between race reports, technical information and human interest angles.

- General works, always written from a particular perspective depending on the author: triathletes (very often elite) journalists (specialist press), coaches (rarely), doctors (often), physical education teachers, etc.

- Scientific articles or similar, quite difficult in their approach (relying heavily, for example, on physiology) and often taken from academic papers or English speaking magazines.

Despite their wealth of content, I was struck by how biased these documents were, giving the reader nothing more than a very restricted view of the triathlon: the pedagogue's advice, the unique experience of the elite triathlete, the doctor's health angle, the energetic and biomechanic reality of the research worker, etc.

In fact, none of these works allowed for a complete understanding from different practical points of view. And that is because no athlete, coach, doctor, teacher, journalist or research worker can pretend to totally embrace the complex and multiple realities of the triathlon…

So the idea came to me to do just the opposite from all my predecessors and not seek to put over my experience, argue my case, or impose my idea of the triathlon.

Quite the opposite. It became important for me to bow down before the evidence (sometimes contradictory), to implicitly suggest that there is not one single line to follow in order to teach, train or practice this sport. Believing in a single, standardised training method highlights part of the heresy. Triathlon is such a complex sport and each athlete who practises it is so different from his training partner that it is left to each one to find their own way, come hell or high water.

This work relies on the idea, simple in itself, yet verified many times over, that two can (very often) be greater than one. The accumulated experience of those who have made a mark in the short history of our sport is irreplaceable and constitutes our most profound cultural heritage. So it was necessary to bring together the different elements in a single document as a means of providing for everyone evidence of the very best that is going on from a practical point of view, at a given moment in our history.

The interviewees are triathletes or coaches all recognised as experts in their field whether through their performances or their extraordinary technical know-how. They are without doubt the best of their generation. The mere mention of their names has resonance for all followers of triathlon: Simon Lessing (Great Britain), Karen Smyers (United States), Luc Van Lierde (Belgium), Isabelle and Béatrice Mouthon (France), Lothar Leder (Germany), Eduardo No Sanchez (Spain), Brett Sutton (Australia), Susanne Nielsen (Denmark), Philippe Martin (Switzerland), Grégoire Millet and Laurent Chopin (France), so many key personalities, so many titles and medals gleaned on the international stage these last 15 years.

These revered giants, encountered by chance during an over busy international calendar, have accepted the always delicate test of submitting themselves to the friendly fire of the inquisitor, delving into their training practices, their habits, both pre and post competition, their closely guarded secrets that fate might have let them keep until the end of their careers. But curiosity conquered all, and the idea of sharing so many riches for the progress of our sport won out in the end, to our great pleasure.

The pages which follow faithfully reflect the tenor of these long conversations, carried out over a period of four years, and which have been grouped thematically, so as to make for more methodical reading. They aim to highlight the practice of each of these giants, to let some of the great certainties of our sport shine through and suggest above all to the reader that you are open books capable of enriching your intimate knowledge of the triathlon, both in training and in competition.

CHAPTER ONE

THE CAST

They are among the Gods of international triathlon. The star athletes are well known: triathletes such as Isabelle Mouthon, Lothar Leder, Karen Smyers, Luc Van Lierde and Simon Lessing. They have excited us, some of them for almost 15 years, by amassing world and European titles, and gaining coverage for our sport through the media all over the world.

We often know less about those who work in their shadows. The coaches, eternal student-researchers, who are obliged, day after day, to re-invent training schedules, concoct new recipes which they adapt to a sport which is like no other. Because, just in case anyone has any doubts, triathlon is not a simple amalgam of the three events of swimming, cycling and running.

Here are some pen portraits of those men and women that ensure that this discipline resembles none other.

Isabelle and Béatrice Mouthon (France, triathletes) are the most famous twin sisters in French sport. As children, they swam and ran for the fun of it. They started in triathlon in 1985, and, after finishing their studies, fashioned brilliant professional careers (Isabelle is a qualified physiotherapist while Béatrice has a degree in town planning). "It was impossible to choose between swimming and running, and because we didn't want to work in a closed, chlorinated environment or on a track, we were attracted towards the triathlon and the wide open spaces".

Their achievements are impressive: Isabelle was double world long distance champion in 1994 and 2000, world champion runner-up in 1997, winner of the Goodwill Games in 1994 and seventh in the Sydney Olympic Games; she was four times European champion, a double winner of the European cup, second in the 1995 Hawaii Ironman, second in the 1995 world cup, third in the world rankings in 1997 and 1998, fourth in the 1991 world championships – and four times fifth (1994-'95-'97-'98). She has also won the French championship more than ten times.

Béatrice won the 1999 French Grand Prix, became national long distance champion in 1994, was sixth in the world championships long distance in 1997 (team world champion), fourth in the European championships in 1995, fifth in the world cup 1992, eighth in the Hawaii Ironman in 1995, 35th in the Sydney Olympic Games... and finally beat her sister at the triathlon in 1999 after 14 years of trying!

Karen Smyers (United States, triathlete) has an economic degree from Princeton. She worked as a consultant in a computer company in Boston before becoming a professional triathlete. An all-round sportswoman, she practised tennis, gymnastics, field hockey and swimming, and entered her first triathlon in 1984 from her athletics club. She broke through in 1989 when she won a place on the US national team and finished fourth in her first world championships in Avignon. Her achievements speak for her; three times world champion (1990-'95-'96) and twice runner-up (1993 and 1994), winner of the 1991 world cup, winner of 1995 Hawaii Ironman and twice second (1994 and 1999).

Lothar Leder (Germany, triathlete), the bad boy of the triathlon. He might well have spent his whole life in a bank had it not been for a long spell in the army (in the sports division) which made him change his mind. He became a professional triathlete in 1994, the year in which he finished second in the long distance world championships. He took part in his first triathlon in 1986, but will be best remembered when, in 1996, in the Roth triathlon he became the first man to break the eight hour barrier (7 hrs 57min 52sec) for the Ironman distance. He won Roth again in 2000 and 2002, was third in the Hawaiian Ironman in 1997 and 1998, and sixth in the 1995 world championship; he was twice German champion.

Luc Van Lierde (Belgium, triathlete) will always be remembered as the man who captured the Hawaii Ironman at his first attempt. Originally a swimmer, he began triathlon in 1989. Second in Europe in 1995, he won the title the following year, during which he was also second in the world championships. His conversion to the long distance confirmed him as one of the greats of the event: 1997 and 1998 world champion (having been second in 1995 and 1996), winner of the 1996 Hawaiian Ironman, when he established his place in history, and 1999, and also of Roth in 1997.

Simon Lessing (Great Britain, triathlete), a journalism student, is beyond question the most elegant of triathletes (1.92m, 74kg) and the most talented the world has yet produced. He started swimming at the age of eight and at 12 started running (track and cross country), before beginning, in 1989, a triathlon career unequalled to this day: five times world champion – in 1992, 1995 (short and long distances), 1996 and 1998, world champion runner-up in 1993 and 1999 (third in 1997), European champion in 1993 and 1994, double winner of the Goodwill Games (1994 and 1998), and four-time winner of the France-Iron-Tour (1994-95-96-97). His only one enormous disappointment: an inexplicable ninth place in the Sydney Olympics.

Susanne Nielsen (Denmark, triathlete) has been swimming from the age of 12 and became a B international 12 years later. But it was the triathlon that brought her most success: she won the European cup three times (1993, 1995 and 1997), was twice third in the European championships (1995 and 1997), a title she won in 1996, and became world long distance champion in 1999.

Brett Sutton (Australia, coach) has his critics but is without doubt the world's best coach. He has picked up a score of titles with a succession of men and women, Australian or not: 15 world champions, world cup winners, European champions, European cup winners and Australian champions. Brett also had three of the athletes he coaches in the first ten in the women's event at the Sydney Olympics, and took the men's bronze medal with the Czech Jan Rehula. His secret? In his family everybody (his father, brother and sister) coaches, and he himself has coached since he was 14. Swimmers (he was national swimming coach for ten years), triathletes, and also racehorses! Brett was also an outstanding sportsman: he played squash at national level and was Australian boxing champion in his weight class! He has coached, or still coaches, world class athletes such as Jackie Gallagher, Emma Carney, Loretta Harrop, Joanne King, Greg Welch, Ben Bright, Greg Bennett, Jan Rehula, Andrew Johns, Markus Keller, Siri Lindley, Jasmine Haemmerle, Annie Emmerson and Nancy Kemp-Arendt.

Grégoire Millet (France, triathlete, now coach) has a brilliant cv: as a competitor he was a top cross-country skier (French Universities' squad, 30th in the Transjurassienne classic), a French triathlon champion and fourth in the 1986 European championships. In winter triathlon, he won the 1988 French championships. He holds a doctorate in the physiological determinents of locomotion in triathlon, and has a range of national sports diplomas. He has been national trainer of all the French squads. In triathlon, he supervised French, European and world champions (Isabelle and Béatrice Mouthon, Sophie Delemer, Anne-Marie Rouchon, Lydie Reuzé, Philippe Fattori), and also coached mountain biker Jean-Christophe Savignoni. In 1998 he became national performance director for the British Triathlon Association, a position he held until the Sydney Olympic Games. Today he is senior lecturer at the University of Montpelier.

Philippe Martin (Switzerland, coach) comes from the world of industry. A construction engineer, he has a real passion for data processing and the computerisation of all his coaching programmes. He has been in turns a wrestler, cyclist, footballer, rower, and waterpolo player – all after Alpine skiing (giant slalom). Aged 18, he became a swimming coach and when one of his athletes asked him in 1988 to prepare him for the triathlon the athlete won and the coach was second! Philippe is a coach to the Swiss national junior team and also supervised the elite from 1994 till 1997. He coached the 1989 and 1990 European junior champion Thomas Leutenegger, who also won the 1990 world junior title; he also trained Olivier Hufschmidt, European and world duathlon junior champion in 1993, before finally advising Simone Aschwanden, the 1997 European champion and the 1998 and 1999 world junior duathlon champion.

Eduardo No Sanchez (Spain, coach), Basque, simultaneously studied physical education at INEF in Madrid and medicine at Santander university. A rower, cyclist and canoeist, he began competing in the triathlon in 1985. Today he is technical director of the Spanish Triathlon Federation (FET), and coach to Madrid based national squad athletes. The Spanish triathletes he coaches have been very successful in recent years: Ivan Rana (the 2002 European champion), Eneko Llanos and Maribel Blanco were, respectively, fifth, 23rd and 24th at the Sydney Olympics.

Laurent Chopin (France, coach) became a professional triathlon coach in 1991 at the Racing Club of France, then in Beauvais, after studying chemistry and applied mathematics. He still coaches many athletes at all levels, including Alexandre Guérin, Cyrille Mazure, Philippe Fattori, Samuel Pierreclaud, Thomas and Marion Lorblanchet, Stéphane Poulat, Cornélia Bourgadel, Sophie Delemer, Xavier Galéa, Vincent Bavay, Marc Simonet, Yves Lossouarn and Nancy Kemp-Arendt (LUX). He is also a consultant in triathlon and running, most notably for Eurosport.

CHAPTER TWO

TRIATHLON, TRIATHLETE, COACH

(Triathlon) it is the classic example of sport where you fight against the elements horizontally, seated, and finally upright, with the aim of overcoming the forces of gravity and fatigue. Isabelle Mouthon.

A great triathlete is distinguished by his consistency in training as much as in competition. Simon Lessing.

As coach you take ten decisions and you hope that seven will be good... A great coach will make three mistakes. A good coach will make six out of ten correct decisions. An above average coach will have a five out of ten success rate. The rest should not be allowed to coach because they risk destroying talented athletes very quickly. Brett Sutton.

I begin this book about the triathlon with an attempt to define what the triathlon is today: a sport practised by two million aficionados of cross training, obsessed with nature and travel; a sport staged in 120 countries, one which has convinced the Olympic movement of its fantastic attraction.

Everyone quoted in this book is going to give their personal definition of the triathlon, their slant on the discipline, their deep motivation, their way of seeing things and their lifestyle. Each of us will recognise something or someone in this account.

Triathletes and coaches will be defined somewhere in these pages, where they will have to answer these fundamental questions: what qualities are necessary for a triathlon champion? Which methods should be followed to become a great coach? This is a dangerous exercise, but one which we all have to succeed at, those of us who open these initial pages of what is an extraordinary professional dictionary.

Brett Sutton

My very first impression of the triathlon remains unchanged: it is an endurance sport that requires total commitment and remains the ultimate challenge for every self-respecting sportsman. The complex technical dimensions of this sport make it a more complete and pure discipline than swimming which is acknowledged as being more explosive.

You become an exceptional triathlete by hard work, and you don't need drugs to get there. If you do not train very hard, you have no chance of success whatever your intrinsic qualities and the scientific and psychological support you can count on. If you do not have as a guiding principle that you are going to work hard to be consistent you have no chance of breaking through in the triathlon.

Because it is a very technical sport, it is necessary also for you to be attentive. I have coached very good athletes who were not particularly talented physically, but who worked very hard and succeeded in activating their mass of slow twitch fibres and in optimising their aerobic capacities beyond all expectation... My innermost conviction remains that, even at sprint distance triathlons (750m swimming, 20km cycling, 5km running, Author's note), triathlon is an aerobic test, and that it is advisable, firstly, to aim at the development of these specific qualities.

To coach in a sport such as triathlon requires an awareness of what I just said. Besides, a big part of the success I have had with my athletes, is because I am always there for their training. I want to see them and smell them. I want to be capable of modifying the schedule immediately. Certain sports sit well with established and very rigid structures with clear directives. I do not think that triathlon falls at all into this category. There are so many elements (fatigue, injuries) which can disrupt even the most careful preparation, leading to readjustments.

So a coach has to be very flexible. He has to permanently observe his athletes and understand both their physiology and psychology. Certain athletes will get more and more tired but will push on in training because they are hard people. The coach has to realise at once when this occurs. It is the one absolute requirement with elite athletes.

Finally, a good coach must know how to communicate with his athletes. He must understand them and make sure they understand what he expects from them.

To be a good coach, then, is to have that feeling that comes with experience, to know how to communicate, but also to know the sport you teach. In this case, it is necessary to master not only aerobic processes, but also the biomechanics of the three disciplines which make up the triathlon. I call them disciplines because they are part of a whole which is inextricably linked. When I began to coach triathlon, I thought that I would coach triathletes as I did my swimmers. But I quickly discovered that my swimming programmes were of no use to me when it came to coaching cycling and running, and that my triathletes were making no progress in any of these two disciplines. You have to mix the ingredients of the three disciplines as if you were preparing a cake: if the mixture is bad, too much of this, not enough of that, the cake is bad. And that is what is so interesting with this sport.

Personally, I find it difficult to argue in black or white terms about triathlon training. I can tell you: I do not know everything. I learn, I experiment all the time with different things. If I tell swimmers, who I think are not very good, to cover 6km, and that they have to cycle and to run later, there's a chance it will destroy them. So what do you do? I can give them 3km, and while I then have no chance of improving their swimming, at least their cycling and running will not be affected. In other words, a triathlete who has a problem with running can have a programme of training completely different from a triathlete who has difficulties with swimming. And that is the beauty of this sport: it is a combination of sports disciplines. It is necessary for us not only to know swimming, cycling and running, but also to be able to integrate their parameters into the triathlon. And this is where I differ from most of the other coaches. I coached an Australian running champion with triathlon methods. And everybody said to me: "You cannot do that". But I did. When my girls are ready to run I could take them to the national athletics championships and they would all reach the 10,000m final.

It is extremely difficult to improve in a discipline when you're no good at it. Everyone leans towards the physiological side, but you must look to the motor skills. It is the reason I always have six athletes following six completely different programmes. And four of the six should make it. As coach you take ten decisions and you hope that seven will be good. Three will therefore be bad. So a great coach will make three mistakes. A good coach will make six out of ten correct decisions. An above average coach will have a five out of ten success rate. The rest should not be allowed to coach because they risk destroying talented athletes very quickly.

You have to have this flexibility, and make sure that your athletes have faith that your decisions will be mostly correct. That is why if they are doing well in racing, they should be congratulated. If they have behaved properly, we have done well. If they missed their way, I am to blame. That is how I see it.

Grégoire Millet

Triathlon? It is above all about 15 years of my life: four years as competitor, and more than ten years as coach! A definition of the triathlon? I love this one: "One sport, two transitions, three disciplines" which is the title of a book published recently (see bibliography at the end of work, Author's note).

The qualities required to become a great triathlete? Physical endurance, naturally! But also the ability to learn, the capacity to be self-contained and have a stable personality. Performance in triathlon is not only connected to the development of energy levels, but also largely dependent on acquiring more or less specific skills. Triathlon should no longer be perceived as a sport for workhorses. I prefer athletes who make their own judgements and who understand things. The development of stamina can be achieved only in the long term and requires enormous motivation to be able to last the course. You have to be able to adapt your technique to minimise the energy expenditure, to train at a high intensity with less effort. It requires the ability to learn. Finally, the capacity to be autonomous is necessary in all sports but it is particularly so in triathlon where a significant part of the training is done without a coach.

A great coach must above all have had experience. In all human activities, expertise is acquired by years of practice (ten at least); therefore it is advisable to learn to work with different athletes, to learn to pursue different objectives and at different times. It is necessary to be able to benefit from scientific and systematic training, not for the sake of research alone, but so as to be able to choose with full knowledge of the facts what is going to improve performance, and also to know how to surround yourself with scientists who can analyse and optimise performance. Furthermore, you have to be passionate about sport. The investment required at a high level is so important that if you are not passionate you cannot succeed. Finally, a good coach is one who has gained the confidence of his athletes and, beyond just listening, must stay on course and see an idea or programme through to the end. The coach is like an artisan who successfully completes from beginning to end a piece of work which is close to him.

Isabelle and Béatrice Mouthon

(Béatrice) It is the management of the three disciplines which make up a complete sport; an intelligent sport combining water, air and ground, and one in which you cannot cut corners.

(Isabelle) it is the classic example of sport where you fight against the elements horizontally, seated, and finally upright, with the aim of overcoming the forces of gravity and fatigue.

The qualities needed to be a good triathlete are first and foremost the mental ones of marshalling in time and space the physical qualities and the technique needed to cope with stress, the external conditions, the other competitors, as well as the spectators. I do not know if there are other sports, apart maybe from adventure endurance, where the management of so many parameters exists.

(Béatrice) You need 40 percent physical endurance and 60 percent mental. You have to cope with three disciplines in three different elements. It is vital to have an overview of your sport and understand what is happening currently as well as what will happen during your career. There's also perseverance and aggression. You must want it badly! You need to know how to do everything for yourself, to be autonomous, to look after yourself. It is not a sport where the coach has to be there all the time.

The coach has to put himself at the same level as the athlete mentally and physically. He must be able to fit in the level of work needed with the personality and lifestyle of the athlete.

(Isabelle) Communication, availability and know-how are the qualities to expect from a good coach. They have to be able to answer the needs of athletes who demand physical, technical or psychological support and need encouragement.

Karen Smyers

Any combination of three sports can be called triathlon, but the best known and recognised is the famous swim-bike-run, at distances varying from a sprint test (less than one hour of effort) to the Ironman (eight or nine hours for the men and women winners). I suppose you also have to include in this definition events where the order is reversed, or back-to-back triathlons.

To be a good triathlete, you can't have any weak points. I succeeded in finishing well (between fifth and tenth place) in many races due to an excellent background in swimming and running, but I could only get to the top by improving my cycling considerably. I would have broken through much earlier if drafting had been allowed in the 1980s! You also have to persevere and be patient (it is really difficult to balance training in three disciplines and not get frustrated so that you neglect one of them or not train enough in a specific sport to become a true specialist). It is necessary to realise the enormous impact each discipline has on the other two. Finally, you have to be aggressive and have this attitude: "Rather death than surrender". Each competition is just like a season, alternating as many highs and lows, so you should never give up.

There were hardly any triathlon coaches when I made my debut. And I think I know more about training (at least as regards mine!) than any other coach today. It is true, now that triathlon is a recognised sport, that there are numerous coaches with a lot of experience who are in a position to prevent a lot of heartache and save all that precious time which I once lost in the crowd... A good coach should possess solid knowledge of physiology as well as nutrition; he must also be capable of identifying quickly any problems, of establishing with his athletes long-term objectives which they should endeavour to fulfil, to tailor training programmes to suit every competitor. That means coaches should have gained a lot of experience.

Lothar Leder

It is a hard sport but fun, characterised by a deal of positive stress and non-stop changes: bang-bang-bang! When I began triathlon, it was adventure with a capital A, and I always wanted to keep this viewpoint. I do not want in any way to throw myself into scientific preparation. Above all I want to continue to enjoy myself.

Qualities needed to be a good triathlete? Above all, stay healthy and avoid injuries; be consistent in training and compete regularly; enjoy training; don't get overexcited, stay cool!

Triathlon is still such a young sport that there are not that many good coaches; let us say that there are five in the world. But there are a lot of coaches around who talk a lot ... My experience has taught me that the best coaches are those that speak least, those that have least scientific knowledge, those that coach by intuition. Ten years ago, it was very difficult to coach triathlon. Now that drafting is allowed it is easier: among other things it let coaches coming from other disciplines adapt more easily. I am my own coach, I use my experience and training diaries to guide me and help me progress. In fact, I had recourse to two coaches in the past. The first was a swimming coach before becoming our federation's national coach. More than a coach, he was a counsellor I could ask questions. Much later (from 1994 till 1996), I worked with a gymnastics coach, with whom I spent a lot of time stretching as well as learning about co-ordination in running. This period, which remained more or less secret, was extremely beneficial to my results. I continued to work with him on and off in 1998. Where preparation is concerned, my wife (the triathlete and duathlete Nicole Mertes, Author's note) is a good adviser. We always talk training. I ask her questions like: "Do you think it is a good idea to do this tomorrow?" She answers, and I can even change my mind. It is what is called a very productive marriage! It is true that I am an extreme kind of guy, and to hear "normal" answers can only do me good...

Luc Van Lierde

In the beginning triathlon was an individual sport. Today there are two triathlons and so there are two definitions of the triathlon: individual triathlon over long distances, and team triathlon over short distances with drafting allowed.

To be a good triathlete... you need to know how to swim. If you do not get out of the water first over short distances you have no chance of shining today. As regards long distances, the priority is mental strength.

To prepare for long distances, a single coach is enough. For short distances, I think that two coaches are necessary: one for general programming and one for specific running training. There is a difference between being a coach and being a trainer. I have the two. The coach follows me on every run, in every hard session, when I train behind a motor-pacer. The trainer is the one who devises the schedule.

Philippe Martin

Triathlon, basically, is a sport like any other, but it is also a lifestyle. It is a completely separate sport, made different by the simple addition of the three disciplines of which it comprises. As for the duathlon, Olivier Bernhard defines duathletes as "Bein Menschen", "Leg men". The duathlon is, according to him, much harder than triathlon.

To be a good triathlete, it is necessary to swim well above all else! If Natascha Badmann (European champion in 1997 and five times runner-up in the European triathlon and duathlon, winner of the Hawaii and Zofingen Ironmen: Author's note) had had the chance of swimming when young, she would be amongst the elite. Swimming is an excellent way to achieve technique and co-ordination. The triathlete must also be ready physically and mentally to take on a big workload, to train more than other sportsmen (more than footballers for example!) and to have intelligence, a balance just as much technical as psychological or social. A future triathlete, for example, would gain by playing handball at sport school.

The essential quality of a good coach is adaptability. He has to adopt a flexible approach, without straying off the line. His approach should be unconventional.

Simon Lessing

Triathlon is not the simple addition of three sports, but a combination of all three: swimming, cycling and running.

I think a good triathlete is strong in all three disciplines. He is multi-talented and must be exceptionally good at swimming and running, but he also has to be strong enough to stay with the leaders or even make the break in cycling. The good triathlete has to work hard in training as well as competition. In preparing for events, he has to force himself through a minimum of five sessions in each discipline each week. As for competition, you can't expect him to win all the time, but he must try to finish among the best each time he competes.

Triathlon is a unique sport in which athletes with incredibly varied profiles compete. They might be very good at one discipline but weaker in another. A good coach has to have this subtle understanding of the event, as well as recognising the strengths and weaknesses of his athletes. Although it incorporates three different disciplines, it is completely different from just the swimming, just the cycling and just the running. And the triathlon coach cannot simply be a swimming, cycling or running coach. The coaches who guide me in swimming and running were all very strongly involved in the sport, and they understand my body and its limits.

Eduardo No Sanchez

Triathlon? Naturally it is the three fundamental disciplines, but it is also an extraordinary passion shared by all the athletes in this unique sport.

Intelligence and patience are the main qualities of the good triathlete. Naturally they also need great athletic qualities, and to demonstrate will-power.

As for the qualities needed by a coach. I would tend to say they are the same as those needed by the athlete: intelligence, patience, will-power, and of course a knowledge of the training needed. A triathlon coach should not completely lose touch with the practices of the sport in order to appreciate with his own body and heart the sensations and feelings which the competitors undergo in training and while competing.

Susanne Nielsen

Triathlon is a personal thing, a battle against the clock in which you fight more against yourself and against time than against your rivals.

Triathletes need different qualities these days compared to a few years ago. Then you had to be strong in all three disciplines. Today it is a question of concentrating more on running and swimming. There are fewer and fewer triathlons like the 1997 European championship in Vuokatti which included a two kilometre hill to be climbed four times in cycling, which meant that good cyclists did not have to save something for the run. Triathlon is a demanding sport which asks a lot of the body. So the triathlete has to have the qualities necessary for these demands: a very strong mind and the ability to confront all the challenges that arise.

To be respected, the coach must be able to earn that respect. They have to be able to impose a strong and solid regime while at the same time being open to your personality and sensitive to how they are going to treat you in order to make you realise what they expect from you. In other words, the coach has to possess the qualities of a psychologist.

Laurent Chopin

Triathlon is defined by its transitions. It is the test of endurance which requires specific physiological and psychological qualities. It is an individual sport, although the introduction of certain rules (notably drafting) has robbed it of a part of its essence. It is also a natural sport par excellence, involving water, air and earth; it is held in a privileged environment, and encourages us to think about the notion of human limits.

The qualities required to be a top triathlete are stamina, in both the physical and psychological sense; the capacity to plan for the long term; self-denial, modesty and humility; the capacity to exceed your limits; the ability to be consistent in performance and in results, in training and competition.

You cannot be a good coach if you are not passionate about the sport; if you do not respect the athletes; if you do not have a technical understanding of the three disciplines which make up the triathlon; if you are not available, if you do not know how to listen and explain to the athletes what is useful and what is not; if you do not have a personalised approach to training, adapted to each of the athletes one coaches and the way they express themselves. Finally, a coach must know how to get his message across, and agree sometimes to put his personal life to one side.

CHAPTER THREE

A CAREER IN TRIATHLON

Success can also be spelt with three Ts: Talent, Toil and Time. Francois Garagnon*

Top level triathletes learn by experience. Top performance does not only correspond to physiological potential. It is this potential brought to bear in a particular context, which is that of a very particular opposition allied to a particular training plan. You have to immerse yourself in this for years to gain any benefit. Grégoire Millet.

Their careers develop perfectly. The athletes accumulate major international victories, gather titles, appear on the covers of the specialised magazines but also feature in general interest newspapers, even snatch precious seconds of TV air-time, sometimes make a lot of money in prizes and advertising contracts.

So what is the recipe for success?

Before opening this chapter on how to plan training, it might first be advisable to sketch an outline of the ideal triathlete's career and to answer these simple and crucial questions: at which age should you begin the triathlon? What main stages should be included? When is maturity reached?

The answers elicited naturally reflect the careers of those asked. They also sometimes depart from it. The coaches' comments are also interesting. They have seen numerous athletes pass through their hands and so have the distance necessary for establishing the likeliest rules for gauging a triathlete's career from the moment he begins to when he reaches a peak.

If you have a child who is already converted to the triple test of the triathlon and you are worried about which stages are needed to take him as far as possible on the road to victory; if you are a curious competitor or coach who wants to get it absolutely right from the start of your protegee's early years: this chapter is for you.

Brett Sutton

The young athlete should begin his career in pre-puberty, so as to optimise the development of his motor skills. Girls should begin at 13 to 14, boys 15 to 16. This is my personal opinion which reflects the facts (most of our best athletes started young), but which differs from that currently held in Australia, which wants athletes to become athletes at a more advanced age. Children should even begin to swim earlier, three times a week, until 13 years of age, which is when their swimming training should become more serious and structured. It is in swimming that the motor skills are the most complex; it is therefore important to begin triathlon with swimming.

There is an annoying tendency to criticise me in my own country, mostly because my approach with the juniors differs from the official one. For example, my juniors spend an enormous amount of time on technique (it is a practice I acquired in swimming) before progressing to a more traditional training programme. So, in running for example, I take them onto the track and they will do 100m repetitions until they know how to run and can be forced into a more regimented schedule with long runs and track sessions and so on. The same approach is valid also in swimming. So, Joanne King, for example, spent the first three months of our collaboration without swimming more than 25 metres at a time. I did everything to put her technique in place. She remains a weak swimmer compared to the world's best, but improved enough to be in with a chance of winning (The Australian became world triathlon champion in 1998. This was the year, it is true, wetsuits were allowed and that always favours the non-swimmers, Author's note). She has to continue putting in the work in this area or risks never winning a major race, at least over the short distance.

I would basically spend the necessary time in that area with those repetitions, repetitions, repetitions as my goal until I am happy, until I feel I can move on with the programme that triathletes will follow. So that preparatory phase is very important and it should be done in the early stages. It should happen also because it minimises injury. I tend to have a lot less injuries than other coaches. I believe it is because we get the technique right first and then I can propose large workloads. Injuries in swimming come from poor technique, I believe that is also happening in running. So we try to make sure they have a very efficient swimming and running style.

I am convinced that one day a 16-year-old will win a world cup race because of the primacy of swimming/running. Of course, I don't think it will happen in the European cup, because the kid would lose at least six minutes during the cycling part! But to answer the question of maturity in triathlon differently, Simon Lessing, Spencer Smith and Miles Stewart all got big wins when they were about 20 to 21. It depends also on the structure of their programme of preparation. As regards maturing at Ironman, I repeat that the triathlete's preparation is fundamentally aerobic, and that the more time you spend in this type of training the better you will get. Under these conditions, I believe that at the age of 26, 27, 28 you should have the base to run a marathon in 2hrs 30min.

A problem which we have in triathlon concerns junior status. In my opinion, too much interest is shown in the junior championships. We have had some excellent winners from the Australian junior ranks, but the simple pressure of winning in this category makes the transition to seniors even more difficult. Different race, different mentality. So I've decided not to place any importance on titles and wins in this category. If my young athletes perform well, I am happy, but I try above all to treat them like seniors. I fix their objectives, aiming to get them into the first ten at the world champ-ionships. If they get there, these juniors will be capable of looking after themselves. It is here that I am maybe a little bit different. Youngsters who are created using a programme specially designed for them never seem to progress beyond the junior category. The comment is equally valid for Australian swimming (my past as national coach has taught me that), which is doubtless why I take this position. Very often, it is the less good junior swimmers who make their presence felt at a senior level. In triathlon, Chris Hill (former junior world champion, Author's note) initially encountered big problems when he entered the senior ranks, but those problems seem to have been resolved now. In contrast, Craig Walton (winner of several world cup rounds in recent years, and world champion runner-up 2000, Author's note) immediately showed he was hungry for victory in the senior ranks, doubtless because he was not made to feel that the junior ranks were an end in themselves. In other words: be careful when you set goals for juniors, they are not completely harmless. As for me, I respect my athletes as juniors and don't let them train too much. And if I enter them in the senior ranks in the European cup, it is not to destroy them, but to protect them: I do not want them so see themselves as juniors. I want them to be conscious of their progression towards the senior ranks.

Grégoire Millet

Athletes with good coaches and a varied training in swimming can begin their triathlon careers relatively late at about 16 to 17. Swimming is a very rich sporting discipline which it is absolutely necessary to practise as soon as possible: sprint, the four strokes etc. During puberty, a heavy training volume will allow the aerobic potential to develop. Dry land exercises, and team sports will complete the training base. Later, at the age of 16-20, you can talk about the triathlon when the athlete is more motivated. Cycling is a discipline which requires a preparation which can only be undertaken from the ages of 15-16. So there is no urgency. The same goes for running, but for other reasons, mostly health (potential damage to cartilages, etc.).

The important periods in the career of a triathlete: from ten to 14 to 15, the young sportsman is in a swimming school, completed with diversified dry land exercises and athletics games; from 15 to 17, swimming is dominant with running gradually increasing; at 17-18 is when a triathlete emerges, training regularly in all three disciplines.

In terms of levels achieved: at 19 to 20, the objective could be less than 10min for 3000m running, and less than 5min for 400m swimming (girls); less than 9min10sec and less than 4min 30sec (boys).

During the whole learning period, technique should be emphasised and a sense should be imparted of the value of learning activities.

The legalisation of drafting has been shown to be beneficial because it helps to limit the recourse to doping in triathlon in the sense that the volume of training in cycling no longer needs to be as great as for a solo effort. Drafting puts into perspective the new parameters which have a direct impact on performance: teamwork, tactics, different techniques.

From the age of 18, an athlete with international aspirations should take part in official international events. These events can be prepared for beforehand by entering international team or relay matches, etc.

Even though an athlete might reach world-level standard from 20 years of age, maturity in triathlon is only reached in my opinion between 25 and 30.

Top level triathletes learn by experience. Top performance does not only correspond to physiological potential. It is this potential brought to bear in a particular context, which is that of a very particular opposition allied to a particular training plan. You have to immerse yourself in this for years to gain any benefit.

Isabelle and Béatrice Mouthon

(Béatrice) There is no precise age for beginning triathlon, but what you must have is a multi-sport culture. When you see little Australians taking out their bike with their surfboard under their arm, and they're capable of doing anything without excelling in any one discipline... That's what is lacking in France, where our elitist culture pushes a child to persevere in a sport from the moment he shows certain qualities, and conditions him to becoming a champion.

From a triathlon viewpoint, aquatic sports must be given priority before puberty. Once a swimming base has been acquired there is really no special age for beginning triathlon. Personally, I am not really in favour of triathlon for young people. It would be better for them to acquire an initial experience of competition in just one discipline, swimming for example, because it is easier to get them hooked. You are more of a fighter when you only focus on one discipline.

You have to wait for children to reach a sufficient level of maturity for them to manage three sports as well as preserve their competitive spirit. So beginning triathlon close to 20 seems to me entirely reasonable and will ensure they continue for many years in the sport as long as you know how to manage their careers.

(Isabelle) I think like Béatrice that sports activities have to be started young with the aim of developing physiological and psychological variety. Try everything from the age of five, organise little triathlons just for fun. I am godmother of a triathlon in the Paris area where one sees kids getting involved. It's certainly very enriching and great fun for them to get to the end of these three events. On the other hand, they should not be pushed into making this sport an academic subject very early on.

You could formalise the career of a young triathlete like this: from five to 12 is the period of try-everything, the multi-sports period; from 12 to 18 they should be pursuing one sport alone, whether it be a triathlon discipline or not (from a triathlon viewpoint it is preferable to develop endurance and practise swimming or running); from 18 years of age you have to really concentrate on the triathlon and develop the qualities lacking in order to attain the highest level possible. That was what happened with us.

We have pushed back the age of maturity each year! Physiologically it has been shown that your VO_2max cannot be improved beyond the age of 30 and that pregnancy can increase your physiological capacity. Australian triathletes have shown that you can reach maturity very early. You can also be very competitive up to the age of 35. That's what is interesting about our sport. Over long distances maturity can come later, but that will however only be acquired with experience over the short distance.

(Béatrice) Maturity also depends on how long we plan to stay in the sport. The life expectancy of an Australian triathlete is possibly not the same as mine if I want to pursue this sport until I'm 40.

(Isabelle) It worries me to see certain triathletes like Joanne King who are very competitive very early on over both short and long distance. She forces herself to sacrifice so much and leaves part of her life behind her and takes the risk of it all catching up with her. She is certainly going to get fed up before long and take note of what is lacking in her life. I sincerely hope for her sake that I'm wrong. She risks maturing between 20 and 25 years of age. I expect to mature between 28 and 33 to 34. One thing is certain: you can't be mature for 15 years. Of course there's Rob Barel, the exception that proves the rule! But mentally he's learned so much...

(Béatrice) To return to Joanne King, she spreads herself about so much, she submits her frame to so many stresses by taking part in Ironmen while preparing for the Olympics that I really ask myself how her skeleton is going to age. I admire her, but in the long term I don't envy her.

Karen Smyers

Triathletes enjoy longevity, especially over the long distance. Since it's difficult to become a good swimmer without devoting a great deal of time to it, children should join a swimming club and stay there during their school years. If they want to compete in summer triathlons I see no problem with that. But they should not dedicate themselves to the triathlon before their early twenties. Those who come to the triathlon with a true swimming past will have no difficulty in doing well. It seems that you can cycle and run much later on in life.

When talent spotting, it should be a priority to identify those swimmers who have running talent, something which may seem quite unusual. Afterwards, it is possible to teach cycling to just about anybody.

I would introduce running little by little, year by year, and then cycling after two years of establishing the running fundamentals.

You cannot deal with the question of maturity in sport without reference to the age at which you started practising it as well as the content of your training programme. It seems you need seven to ten years of practice before you attain your peak in triathlon. With intelligent training and by taking special care of your health the effect can be cumulative, above all over the long distance where you can increase endurance for about 15 years.

Peak performance should be reached around 28 to 30 years of age over the short distance and 32 to 35 over the long distance. I really have no idea of what effect gender has on the age of reaching maturity in triathlon.

Personally, I don't think I've yet reached full maturity over the short distance. I believe I can go still faster. Especially in cycling where I need to explore new training techniques which would let me, I believe, gain in leg strength. At the same time I think I can maintain my swimming level and still improve on my running (although I've reached a plateau these last six or seven years I've still managed to beat some of my personal bests, for example over five miles.)

Lothar Leder

The career of the triathlete should begin very early, let us say at about 12 years of age, with the aim of being as fast as the pros by 18 so that you can enjoy a good career. But the most difficult stage will still be the transition from junior to professional.

Swimming should be taught from the youngest age (If I could turn the clock back to when I was young I would swim more). But running should equally be taught and even more so today given the importance it has on the way races are run.

Good basic training is fundamental, without interval training, when you are young. I started with basic endurance. In fact, neither the sport practised nor the time devoted to it, nor the structure of your training programme matters, as long as you practise basic endurance and take great pleasure in what you do.

A problem you come across today concerns the number of triathletes who run more and more at an earlier age. They lose their enjoyment in training, a little like swimmers who lost interest in swimming and end their careers at the age of 20. Triathlon is a sport where you can compete very late on

Young people should not consider Ironman. Not too soon. It kills athletes: you are tired and you get injured from one moment to the next.

So, the 12 to 18 age range should be that of basic endurance. When that has been optimised, young athletes can run and increase the intensity of training, and competition will not harm them as much. Thanks to a consistent endurance base hard intervals can be carried out without difficulty. Basic work does not mean high mileage. It can mean one hour running or two to three hours cycling.

I don't think there's a specific age for reaching a peak in your career. You can reach it at 18 like Benjamin Bright, or at 35 when you run an Ironman. Joanne King is a good example of an athlete who started her career over the long distance very early (she has been criticised severely for this), but I don't think her transition to the long distance was premature. And although her level is already excellent (she has already won the Roth

Ironman, Author's note) she will gain in stability over the long distance and will notch up a number of good wins if she does not get injured.

I no longer think there is any special difference in reaching maturity between men and women, although the junior women are faster earlier. This is certainly due to the fact that they can take harder training when they are younger. But that's maybe because they complain less than the boys.

Luc Van Lierde

Triathlon is a very hard sport, demanding a great deal of time spent adapting to it. In my opinion a minimum of five years is needed to adapt. I remember my early years when I was injured two or three times each year. Basically, it is an advantage if you come from swimming, but on the other hand you get injured a lot. In any case it is important to increase mileage very progressively during this period and not take part in too many competitions.

Depending on your original sport and the type of triathlon you want to compete in, training priorities are different. In my case, being a swimmer from the start, my priorities naturally veered towards cycling and running.

Most triathletes began their career as swimmers. I think it's a mistake to start triathlon too early, like in certain countries where they start at ten to 12 years of age. For me, the most ideal age is 16 to 17.

Maturity is both physical and mental. Physically, maturity takes longer because years of training are needed. Mentally, the balance is very delicate and involves motivation. An athlete who has been at the top for a long time and has accumulated victories from his first years in the sport may no longer be able to motivate himself. So maturity is a very complex phenomenon.

You have to begin by practising short distance triathlon. And when your body has adapted to it, you can attack the long distances. From this perspective, maturity appears later over the long distance compared to the short. This means that to prepare for the long distances you have to prepare over the short, and the opposite is also true. To compete over long distance at the end of the season you have to rely on a speed base that has been built up over the course of the season. On the other hand, if you want a short distance season, you can take part in a long distance event at the start of the year, since in any case you need mileage in triathlon.

Philippe Martin

I have two very young children. The girl will be a tennis player and the boy a golfer! No, let's be more serious, I advocate a very diversified approach, multisports, until ten to12 years of age. From this age on, knowing how to swim becomes a priority; that is, learning the technique. Triathlon should only become a speciality at around 18 to 20 years of age. So chronologically, the swimmer should come before the (Bein Mensch) Leg Man.

The golden age in triathlon (as in duathlon) is between 25 and 30 years of age. For long distances, it is about 30 years of age.

I coach juniors. Does that mean I don't make them do very much? It's a cruel dilemma! As coach to Swiss juniors, I have to make sure that my triathletes are above all good juniors, while at the same time creating the conditions for a future blossoming of talent. That means, that in national junior teams, the important thing is to build the future. It is not vital for them to be excellent cyclists or runners. You have to bet on the long term, on the margin of progress for each one.

Simon Lessing

To succeed in triathlon you have to start to be interested around 14 to 15 years of age. Young people should adopt a multisport philosophy. It seems important to me to grow up as a triathlete and not just come from swimming and throw yourself into cycling and swimming at around the age of 18 to 19.

If it is important to grow up practising the three disciplines, the aim is not quantity but rather to generate the conditions for a cross training effect since the body should adapt to the different pressures which are put on it during a triathlon.

It is best to begin swimming very early, giving priority to the technical side of things that need to be acquired. It is the same for running because it is seen as crucial to expose the body to the specific shocks connected to this activity so that it can adapt.

The general rule should be: not too much too soon. A general involvement within the sport is necessary in the early building stage, when pure enjoyment must prevail over competing. Specialising should start at the age of 18, 19 or 20 (Sprint and Olympic distance), in such key aspects as technique and speed work.

From 21, 22 to 30 you simply need to maintain the technique and speed that you have built in the preceding phase, when your body has developed, grown and adapted to the different changes specific to performing a triathlon.

As for me, I have never spent time training to prepare for a long distance triathlon. I competed twice in the Nice event (4km swim, 120km cycle, 30km run, Author's note) and that's my only outing over long distance to date. My training is relatively short and intensive. I have never had this German philosophy where lots of mileage is the solution. I get away with very little weekly mileage: 15 to 18km swimming, 250 to 300km biking, 60 to 65km running.

Don't try to become world champion at the age of 15. Your time will come in your early twenties. Simply enjoy the sport.

Over short distances, you reach maturity between 24 and 30 years of age. Your biological clock teaches you that it is difficult afterwards to keep up much longer the type of intensive work required for the short distances. Your performances take a dive, even if you may still improve your endurance. Personally, I have not yet experienced that, but I suppose my time will come.

Over the last couple of years, I have had to adapt my training. Maybe I am not recovering as quickly as I used to when I was 18 to 19 years old. I sometimes need two days to recover from a hard session when I previously only needed one day. What experience teaches is not to get locked into a single train of thought, to be ready to listen to others, to understand and then adapt to the changes which are not only taking place in your body but also in your sport.

Eduardo No Sanchez

The career of an athlete should begin in the swimming pool. Contact with the water is crucial, well before the age of majority, but not necessarily in a team or even in competition.

Several stages should be included in the long-term planning of a career: an initial playful phase which is indispensable for preserving a lasting interest in sport; next, serious involvement in an activity, at least in competition, in order to discover the constraints of the sporting environment and get involved voluntarily in a serious project; finally, you have the practice of triathlon proper.

It is still difficult today to speak about the age of maturity in triathlon because the generations of athletes that succeed each other are stronger earlier. The juniors I train today are much more competitive than some years ago and are already as strong as our current elite.

That said, I think that at the present time athletes competing over the Olympic distance mature at around the age of 25 to 26. Those are the only ones who interest me, professionally speaking.

Susanne Nielsen

An athlete's career should really start at around 18 years of age, at the end of a period of a progressive build up which might be started at around the age of 15. The mistake many make is to do too much too soon. Many youngsters do an enormous amount of training and sadly disappear at the end of three or four years, over-trained, tired and demoralised. Swimming and cycling may be pursued sooner than running which is the most traumatic of the three. If I had to plan young triathletes' careers they would certainly start with swimming, but not intensively, because it is important above all else for a youngster to start his career mentally and physically fresh and with the soul of a conqueror.

A triathlete's career can be more or less long, depending on its aims and how long his motivation remains intact as well as the other priorities in his life, like how much time he should dedicate to his family, for example. One cannot in fact plan the end of a career. An athlete's career ends at the minute he feels the need or obligation and not because it was programmed in ten years earlier.

Even though some reach a high level earlier today, women seem to attain sporting maturity between 28 to 35 years of age, partly because triathlon is an endurance sport and this quality can be optimised later on in life.

Laurent Chopin

Triathlon is the grouping together of three different sports, each possessing its own particular physique, psychology and technique. It requires a not inconsiderable investment in time and money. It requires a certain autonomy and maturity. Therefore, it does not seem to me necessary to start between the ages of eight and ten as in other sports.

That means that a 25-year-old weightlifter has more trouble being competitive in triathlon than a swimmer of the same age. In other words, if it's a kid's vocation to be a triathlete, it would be in his interest to start swimming as soon as possible so that he can acquire the basic, indispensable swimming techniques, in so far as the older he gets the more difficult it is to acquire them.

So, from the perspective of triathlon coaching, it would be preferable to acquire the basic swimming techniques before broaching the two other techniques in a progressive and applied way. This approach will be favoured by the transfer of physiological qualities which will now operate naturally and allow the youngster to cycle and run without any big problem, a playful change much easier than the approach in cycling and running.

I am against premature specialisation. Affirming that the basic techniques of swimming should be taught in the first instance does not mean, in a triathlon school, that it is necessary to proscribe all other sports like, for example, team sports. Thanks to them, the young run and manage their bodies spatially, find their place alongside colleagues and against rivals, all indispensable conditions for the harmonious development of a young person.

The young are always on the move. They do sport at school, in gym and in the playground. The only real shadow over the physical activity of the young is, in fact, swimming!

My message is crystal clear: let's not make our youngsters specialise too soon. Let us make them love sport above all. Triathlon is a sport for mature people. Let's not be too hasty...

As far as sporting maturity goes, the models we have available for reference from other sports are difficult to apply to the triathlon. Firstly, because this is a young sport and we don't have sufficient statistical background to test the models. Then, because triathlon is a combined sport, which brings together three very different disciplines, this makes a model-study almost impossible.

Moreover, I have to admit that I don't like models, because I think that predetermined systematic training cannot be satisfactorily applied to the management of an individual.

In fact, I think that the man on the ground, who should be a coach, has no need of rigid models that he should act on.

Let us take as a rough example two juniors of equal talent. The one is a committed student, the other a full-time triathlete. Who can say which of the two will be the better senior? The answer's not easy. It includes multiple data, at the heart of which the athlete's equilibrium occupies an important place. On the other hand, you can guess, without being too wide of the mark, who will be the better junior.

Let us now take the example of a swimmer who started swimming at the age of six to seven. If he joins a triathlon school at 14, he has eight years of swimming behind him. Under these conditions the technical aspects of swimming have already been absorbed, and he is also physiologically well equipped. It will therefore be necessary to immediately guide him towards learning the other two disciplines. The approach will be presented in completely different terms for another youngster of the same age who started out cycling or running.

In any case, if you accept the logic of a career model then at least one rule becomes apparent: the previous acquisition of all the fundamentals and basic techniques of sporting activity.

My approach is technical and qualitative, based on intuition. My point of departure is the proven principle that physiological qualities will be all the better developed, the greater the technical background.

The technocrat-theorists claim that a sprinter matures long before an endurance athlete. Practice has shown to what extent this statement is wrong. It was not so long ago that people thought that the career of a swimmer reached its peak before the age of 20. Statistical data of the average age of Olympic swimming medallists from Atlanta have demonstrated exactly the opposite is true. On the other hand, if we examine the sporting and social swimming environment of yesteryear and today we will have more answers to the question of maturity in sportsmen.

But so many parameters have to be taken into consideration that it is very difficult to propose a general rule in this matter.

(*) François Garagnon, *Bréviaire de l'homme d'action,* 1990.

CHAPTER FOUR

PLANNING TRAINING

The planning of training is the result of a judicious mix distilled from the varied knowledge of a coach's experience… or the athlete's, if he holds his destiny in his own hands.

Planning, programming, objectives, macrocycles, mesocycles, microcycles, workloads, recovery… so many specialist terms, the nuances of which are not always understood.

Numerous authors refer to and make recommendations in the field of training theory and methodology, explaining their theoretical practice using this sometimes pompous terminology. Or a not always practical theory for those who use it in their sports halls or on their machine…

The purpose of this chapter is to try and take a clearer look at the way the world's best triathletes organise their training, how their race calendars are structured, how they manage their bodies on a day-to-day basis, during the week, for a season or an entire career.

Athletes and coaches use their own jargon and distil theory from what they practise, helping us find our way through this extremely complex maze. They recount how their aims are clarified, how their training programmes are drawn up, how they thrash out the cycles governing their training and illustrate everything with practical, concrete and varied examples. A goldmine for us all, a mouth-watering prospect for any self-respecting coach or ambitious athlete.

Brett Sutton

The first rule is you don't want to risk losing what you have gained from your previous training. We try to have a spiral system in place. When we risk, we want to risk 20 to 25 percent of what we gained, we don't want to go back to nothing. My athletes won't take off four weeks completely.

What we try to do within our programming is to work on the three disciplines at all times. Triathlon is triathlon and I don't believe in resting one of them for a week or two. I know with swimming, that for someone who is a non-swimmer (this is also valid for swimmers of national calibre) to have three weeks of hard training and then one week of rest, as is done in Europe, does not work. They don't rest, they lose the motor learning skills that took three weeks to develop. So we would still do some hard swimming. Even if the kilometres were down, we would still do some anaerobic swimming. Swimming is different to running because there is not the weight-bearing difficulty. It is similar to cycling, we don't have the injury problem. And we also need to feel the water much more than we need to feel our running. So if you back your speed off

---

completely in swimming for more than 72 hours, you find that your athletes start to lose dramatically their feel for the water.

What I basically do is look at the different distances in a way that when we work on one particular thing on one day, for example when we work biking and running in a transitional stage, then the next day we'll work harder on the swim. So we would tire the arms on one particular day and have more recovery with the bike and run, and the next day it will be hard on the bike and run and the recovery will be for the swim. If I have the opportunity, we do the swim last, and use the swim as recuperation before a race. I like to swim after we run, because I think it works on recovery.

So (and this probably distinguishes me from most of my colleagues) I sincerely believe that you have to have recourse to quality work in all the preparation phases. So, each week, my athletes do at least one quality session per discipline, even in a recovery period. Quality, for me, means 25 to 30 beats under maximum heartrate frequency.

In Australia it is different from Europe. In fact we have to do two seasons, the southern hemisphere season and the northern hemisphere. So the first thing I have to take into consideration is that athletes will have to peak twice, once for the Australian season and also be able to back up before the start of the world cup season. I found that some of the Europeans have big problems when they come to Australia and try to go from a long season to two seasons. It is not the problem of getting tired, it is the problem of their bodies that are not used to doing two race seasons, which is not natural for the athlete. We in Australia have to put up with it, and have to regulate our season. For my own part, I have decided to base myself in Europe and not give too much importance to the Australian season. I think that to be more competitive in the future we will basically have to do the European season, so as to regulate our training and reach our peak in the month of September and not in April any more.

I insert recovery stages in the middle and at the end of each work cycle. In general we programme seven to ten day cycles, in the middle of which are included half or whole day rests and at the end of which are observed a two-three day period of relative rest (retaining the volume but reducing the intensity). An athlete will do for example four work sessions and then enjoy a recovery session in which he will do nothing. Then he will embark on another four work sessions with a recovery session etc...

Here is the plan and general rule... Now, the periodisation of the recovery phases within work cycles depends, in fact, on the athlete's profile. For Greg Bennett, who is a sprinter, a recovery phase comes after only a few work phases. It's completely different for Andrew Johns (European champion 1998 and 2000, world and European cup winner 1999, Author's note) whose extreme endurance allows him to do several work phases before complete rest is programmed in. Then you have Markus Keller who, because he weighs ten to 15 kilos more than Greg or Andrew, needs more recovery than the others. These are three good reasons for not following the absurd European rule that one week of relative rest should follow three weeks of intensive work!

In Australia, we have always improvised our training because we don't have a training centre, nor a full-time structure. So we have to permanently adapt our programmes, work and recovery to the fragmentary structures to which we've got access.

If some athletes don't want the rest periods I give them, I always come to an agreement so that they end up obeying. I have the firm conviction that athletes are always stronger at the end of the season if they have been able to agree to these recovery phases at the very heart of programmed work cycles, than if they had continued to train throughout the whole year without stopping.

I try to maintain what I call a healthy line, in relation to which the greater the amount of surplus training, the greater will be the chances of over-training.

One training session a day is sufficient to prepare for short triathlons (promo, sprint or even Olympic). Even competitive triathletes can keep to this programme, some sessions possibly including two sports: running and swimming or cycling and running. If I had to train age-group Australians I would try to explain to them: with an hour-and-a-half a day devoted to the triathlon it would be better for them to concentrate each time on two activities rather than one, in order to establish their technique more efficiently. Then, moving up to the Olympic distance and progressing towards the elite, they should devote at least 15 hours a week to it, 24 maximum.

My preferred distance is Nice. It is much fairer and gives a cyclist the chance of winning the event by making victory impossible if you have a real weak point in one of the three disciplines. On the other hand, in Ironman a good runner can realistically make up for a lapse in swimming or cycling and win the event. Those last 12 kilometres are very long...

As regards the schedule for the long distance, I will incorporate into the short distance a long run every ten days maybe, and a long ride (180km or five to six hours) and in these ten-day cycles I will add a brick which could consist of 140km bike and a 20km run. Some athletes are capable of fitting this into a seven-day cycle, but I admit the idea does not appeal. The long sessions would be too close together. I know that many cyclists use long-slow distance on the bike. It's not part of my mentality (I'm not from one of those countries where cycling is king) to sit in the saddle six hours a day. Cyclists hardly do that in Australia... I really think that it is possible to do short and long distance in the course of the same season if you monitor your training properly.

In terms of goals, the first rule is not to set yourself impossible objectives. The goals depend on the potential and qualities of each athlete. If we are really talking about the elite, I think the ultimate goal for those men and women who consider themselves as such, should be to become world champion, and to be the best a certain number of stages should be successively reached. It is unreasonable to launch yourself prematurely onto a circuit which does not yet correspond to your level.

One of the problems we should face up to at the present time is that there are athletes in the world cup who should not be there and who gain nothing by being there.

All they get is bad results and totally lose confidence in themselves. To get away from that, they should only do events that correspond to their true level.

In triathlon, as elsewhere, there are different types of goals. For example, if you want to get out of the water in the leading group, you have to be able to swim at a given speed. Let's take Jackie Gallagher (Australian world champion 1996, Author's note): she would have to swim under five minutes for 400m. So we set this as a specific target. Similarly, you may want the girls in your charge to be capable of cycling a time trial for 40km under the hour. Or that 10km should be run at a given pace that will of course vary according to each athlete: 33min for Emma Carney (Australian world champion 1994, Author's note) but 37min for Beth Thompson (GBR, European junior champion 1998, Author's note). Then let's take Loretta Harrop (Australian world champion 1999, Author's note): when she started the triathlon in 1996, she was worth 50min over 10km: we set ourselves different level objectives in running between 1996 and 2000 and our goal of the Olympics: 42min, 40min, 38min, 37min, 36min 30sec, with the final goal of running 35min 50sec in the Games. With a time like that, it would be necessary for one of the girls behind to run a record time of around 33 minutes in order to catch her...

In goal terms, I refer to absolute times and not to courses because each circuit is different in triathlon. The only time worthy of attention in a given triathlon is the difference in time between the men and women, a time which will obviously be more significant if the course is hilly than if it is flat. I have been to triathlons where the best swimmer got out of the water in 14min and others where they came out in 22min... To focus on time without putting it into context is a nonsense: you end up being disappointed by a course which has produced an average time although you've run well, or the opposite where you go wild over a record time for a run although the circuit is only 9.5km or less.

To an athlete who wants to be world champion, I suggest that if they can swim this time, bike this time and run this time, they will be world champion. So we set the times in that way, bearing in mind how important the physical and technical profile of the athletes are in time setting. If we take Emma and Jackie, for example, one is a much stronger girl on the bike, while the other is more technically proficient. Jackie is as good if not a better technical rider than all the Europeans I have seen, she would eat them on a standard course. On the other hand, put Emma on a straight 20km ride, and she will ride with the guys. So obviously their goal times have to be different and realistic for each girl.

How many objectives should you set in one year? It's a good question that I have never considered. We identify our aims first, the world championships, and think about what we will have to do to get there. To repeat the preceding example, Emma is a girl who enjoys winning, she always concentrates on each race, while Jackie makes fun the whole time. She can finish seventh in Chicago, but in her case there is nothing seriously wrong. She returns to Australia to train and I take charge of her after four weeks, for the eight weeks that remain up to the world championships. She operates on 70 percent of her potential for 90 percent of the season, concentrating all her energy on one race. That's how she prepares and is successful. Her goals therefore are different. I have encouraged her to come and join us in Europe in our training camp. She has refused, preferring to run in Chicago, go on holiday, go to the Philippines or Japan and do a little training (swimming a lot all the same). At the same time, Emma will prepare very professionally for all her races and will be incapable of standing on the start line, whatever race it is, if she doesn't feel ready to win.

If we had established ourselves permanently in Europe and if we had only one season of races per year, I would still divide the season up into two blocks of 12 weeks, with one race-goal in week six for which I would demand good results and another race at the end of the first cycle (either the end of June or beginning of July, Author's note). Then we would have a break. Then the second cycle would begin, aiming to be in form once again in September.

I think the classical division in macrocycles-mesocycles-microcycles is less relevant in triathlon than in any other sports. Because we have three technical sports.

If you have a technical or motor-learning skill problem in one of the sports, which everybody does, if you have a recuperation period within that particular sport, you tend to lose the motor-learning skills that you picked up with your previous training. I know that in swimming for example, there is nothing worse than having a week of build-up, a week of hard work and a week of rest for a non-swimmer, simply because they do not have the background that swimmers have with six to eight years of motor skill patterns trained. It is the same with running: if you are Philippe Fattori or Greg Welch you can run only three or four times a week and your skill level is excellent, and your conditioning is still stable. You can still be very efficient because you have a running background. If you are Robin Brew or Benjamin Sanson and run three times a week, you are not going to pick up the skills and hold them. That's possibly why so few triathletes really improve their weak points.

So, good swimmers will be certain of a good recovery period in swimming with me; but if they are weak runners, they will still run, and when the intensity is reduced in the programmed recovery period, the mileage is still maintained.

So, we have a mesocycle going and we keep it going by including recovery phases adapted to the moment, profiles and levels of the athletes. In terms of mesocycles, I proceed with the following chronological division: leading cycle, aerobic cycle, attack cycle (in the course of which we work very hard), and finally the competition phase. In the course of each of my mesocycles, each element of the training cycle is changed in relation to the others with the exception of the weak point of each athlete.

Thus, if we are in the middle of the aerobic phase I will retain the intensity element in running if they are mediocre runners, even if at the same time they are good cyclists and swimmers. On the other hand (still in the aerobic phase) if they are bad swimmers, the intensive work will be continued in swimming.

In the attack cycle the triathletes will work hard in any case in all three disciplines.

In the course of the recovery phase after the objective test, they will recover in their favourite disciplines. So, if they're good swimmers and bad runners, they will swim once or twice a week but will maintain their work rhythm in running.

The attack cycle can be a four-week period when there will be hard work in each of the three disciplines. On one particular day, the major emphasis will be on swimming, the next day it will be biking and the next day will be running. And that will roll on right through the cycle. Of course, the order and period may change. I have to play with the training facilities, for example. But if I had to run on two consecutive days, I would not run the same way twice. We would do aerobic one day, and a little bit faster the next day, and a longer slower run the next day, etc. So we have a cycle within each cycle. In swimming, we could swim 15 beats below max, the next day would be 35, and the next day would be 40. So we would keep revolving that around, we would keep revolving the bike around, and we would keep revolving the run around. So there are many cycles rolling around in my head!

Grégoire Millet

A coherent plan of training should respect certain important principles:

The progression principle, right through adolescence, but also in the junior category and in the course of the initial years as senior;

The alternating principle, between work and rest, between physiological pathways, between technical work and muscular work, between central adaptation and peripheral adaptation etc.

The principle of transfer, which reflects the whole problem of cross training, to the interplay of central-peripheral adaptation. This is what forms the basis, in my opinion, of our specificity and the logic of programming in triathlon. I think the specificity of our discipline (and what we can bring to other disciplines) lies more in cross training, in our macroscopic approach than in the strict understanding of the succession of disciplines in the strict sense of the term.

In fact, several important questions inform the whole planning of training. Among them: how to improve in one discipline by working in another? Or again: what are the connections between aerobic development and improved muscle strength?

You can swim in a promotion triathlon and finish it in good condition without training, as long as you know how to swim.

To prepare for the Olympic distance, a minimum amount of training is regarded as necessary (two to four sessions a week): two weekly swimming sessions, one or two cycling (in summer) and one or two runs.

To prepare for the long distance, you must include from time to time long sessions in your training: for example, to take part in the Nice triathlon in September, some long sessions in the summer should be enough. With running, on the other hand, you have to bank on consistency from winter onwards because you cannot increase the loads suddenly. You would risk getting injured. So you have to envisage a minimum of three runs per week.

At an elite level, 20 to 25 hours of training are seen as necessary in order to succeed over the short distance (Sprint and Olympic): 20 hours for the juniors and the initial senior years, 25 hours for older athletes. For long distance, the volumes are more in the order of 25 to 30 hours, or even more during certain specific cycles.

All triathletes are persuaded to consider the coming season with regard to their objectives. For an elite athlete that could be the European or world championships or the Hawaii triathlon, for example. These goals are written into a logic connected to the career plan of the athlete, to the fact that they demonstrate a real desire to take part in these events and that they feel ready to turn in a great performance. It is also necessary to take the organisation of the season as such into account, in a way that it isolates the necessary stages in order to prepare for the goal correctly.

The world cup is not an objective in the proper sense of the term. It is imposed on the international elite in order to enter and remain in a hierarchy so as to qualify for the world championships or the Olympics. We use it more as a means of a high level apprenticeship, allowing us to attain the higher objectives that we are pursuing. Expressed otherwise, you could say that the world cup is formative (it does not matter very much in itself whether an athlete finishes ninth or tenth) while the world championship sanctions the success or otherwise of your preparation. In this way, an athlete who wins a medal in an international championship is completely different in my eyes to one who comes fourth, or another who regularly finishes in the same top places... the athlete who often competes and always finishes in the same place is to my way of thinking an athlete who trains badly. The quality of training is solely evaluated by the objectives which are set.

As a coach, I feel liberated vis-a-vis an athlete who wins an international medal. Then we have both fulfilled our contract.

In my opinion, only one or two result-goals (in competition) and one technical or methodological objective in each discipline can reasonably be set in the course of a season. For example, in cycling, the aim might be (for a junior girl) to ride 60km without any problems, or to be technically more at ease in the pack.

A season is planned with reference to the major championships. The long and necessary period of preparatory work, as well as the training camps (at altitude for example), are fitted in with regard to these objectives. A large part of the timetable is discussed before the season starts, but you never decide too far ahead.

Optimally, there should be a period of five months basic preparation from

December to April. But international calendars no longer allow for this. Athletes won't last ten years finishing their season at the end of November and opening it again on April 15. We are going to have to choose, because a truncated basic preparation does not create the conditions necessary for optimising athletes' potential. You have to stop for a sufficiently long time in order to rest and regenerate, do long work, and embark on a new competitive season. You have to be able to decide not to begin as early as everyone else.

In my opinion, a yearly programme with two peaks does not work in triathlon, or at least is seen as dangerous. You can envisage, for example, running in the course of the months of April and May, then resting in June-July, and beginning again in August with a view to the world championships, but to my meaning the programme is faulty. I find it a bit unrealistic betting on two aims in the same season: the Europeans in July, for example, the worlds in November. In this case, the world championships operate more as remedial work.

It is very important that the annual date of the European championships should be clearly fixed at the beginning of July to let the coach work in peace. The dream now would be to fix the world championships each year at the end of August – beginning of September (which was the case in 1998 and 1999 with Lausanne and Montreal, Author's note)…

The hypothesis of the European championships in July and the worlds in September would allow for one big period of competition which would therefore contain two objectives.

I am for a one-peak periodisation because I see many advantages in terms of apprenticeship and of the effective development of qualities, with a view to optimising the athlete's potential so that they progress from one year to the next.

Globally, the content of work cycles is organised with regard to the following reference paces:

Pace 1, slow continuous work, basic, aerobic capacity.

Pace 2, low: fast continuous work, threshold training or a little below.

Pace 3, high: mixed training, aerobic interval training.

Pace 4, maximum aerobic speed, essentially viewed as intermittent aerobic work, on a foundation of slow-short intervals.

Pace 5, (not touched on in triathlon) lactic and speed work.

Initially, I was considering a model which contained eight different paces. But this model was seen to be inoperative in practice and unworkable with regards to the athlete. The model based on paces 1-2-3 works better, even if it is less precise.

It seems important to me to speak of intensity from the moment training resumes. In fact, the base period no longer exists, properly speaking, which may seem paradoxical with the long preparation period that I have mentioned. From the first weeks of training, you have to start with a cycle of maximum strength and development of maximum aerobic power, accompanied by a great deal of technical work, in such a way that quality of motion does not suffer.

In terms of paces (let's take running as an example), maximum aerobic power should be broached from the onset of winter (pace 3 according to our terminology). Progressively, you have to pass to the group pace (average aerobic training) in the shape, for example, of 1000m repetitions, and continuous fast work, for example over 20mins. In this way the athlete should be capable of carrying out a greater proportion of his training at specific speeds (that is to say, competition pace). You should, however, keep up maximum aerobic speed sessions (speed corresponding to attaining maximum oxygen consumption or VO_2max, Author's note).

In running, it seems to me that it is the adjustment of speed which should direct training.

In cycling, on the other hand, the problem is otherwise, more connected to the muscular sphere, with, as a corollary, the need to alternate the pedalling frequency (muscle/velocity reinforcement). For me it is important to favour specific muscle reinforcement on the ergocycle or on the road.

In swimming, I work on three levels of intensity as well as on all the problems of co-ordination which are regarded as crucial in this discipline.

In terms of the duration of cycles, the following organisation can very schematically be envisaged: a three-week recovery period; eight to ten weeks concentrating on maximum aerobic power and maximum aerobic speed and maximum muscular strength work; these are preferably six-week periods during which progress relies on continuous fast work, for example.

In parallel, more specific work should commence about ten weeks before the dates of the main objectives.

The greatest volume should come towards the end of February and the beginning of March.

It is not really the intensity or the type of work, but rather the volume which marks the difference between the short and long events. Apart from that, there is not a great deal of difference in planning between the short and long distances in triathlon. In concrete terms, 30 hours seems to be a reasonable limit in weekly volume.

In long distance, the frequency of running sessions should be greater and include some long runs (up to 25 to 28km). Isabelle (Mouthon), for example, never ran more than 80km a week when she was preparing for Hawaii (see below Isabelle and Béatrice Mouthon's preparation for Hawaii in this same chapter, Author's note). In cycling, long sessions are really necessary: five hours in the saddle to prepare for Nice, seven hours for Hawaii.

(Isabelle) The key word in all planning for training is progression: progression in

Isabelle and Béatrice Mouthon

your career as well as throughout the year and that training loads and intensity be taken into consideration. Many triathletes who want to imitate the big champions, miss this essential point, which they pay for more or less in the long run.

It is also necessary to start with endurance work, without which you are not in with a shout after two races, or you do not manage to get through the difficult sessions.

For me the picture of training is a pyramid whose fundamental base is endurance into which you progressively inject intensity. And in the course of a year several pyramids are superimposed which implies each time a return to relative long and slow cycles.

(Béatrice) In a training plan, you begin with a break. There are many triathletes who go from one season to the next without recovering. We don't think it's healthy not to give our bodies a break of at least a month. Which does not mean a complete break from sport, you engage the mechanism with a little running or swimming. But you don't go back into it, you recharge the batteries and take pleasure in practising sport.

Then you can recommence calmly the base work with progressive increments of the loads over two months before broaching more specifically into triathlons with interval training.

The work becomes more qualitative as you approach the competitive period. Today, the seasons are so long that you have to create another pyramid in the middle of the year in order to create a new springboard. And recover well. We forget all too easily that rest is a sports period. We say that because with age we spend more time recovering. And he who wants to travel far looks after his mount…

(Béatrice and Isabelle)

To prepare for a long distance triathlon the vital important minimum is 12 hours a week, regularly without fail for eight months, to prepare for an Ironman (less for Nice). It is advisable, furthermore, to pay attention to base work cycling training as a priority without it being too traumatic. Half the training time (six hours) should be given over to cycling and the rest (2x3 hours) divided equally between swimming and running. An elite triathlete, on the other hand, should train at least 30 hours a week to prepare for an Ironman, with the same division per discipline as that suggested for a beginner.

A triathlete should be able to finish his first Olympic triathlon honourably on eight hours a week training and with a division of disciplines perhaps a little different to that for the long distance: here you can, in fact, envisage a rotation of priorities from one week to the next.

(Béatrice) As for fun triathlons, three or four hours of training a week should be enough. Afterwards everything depends: a bad swimmer should maybe spend more time in the water. As with the Olympic distance it will be doubtless necessary to alternate the dominant disciplines…and above all enjoy it!

(Isabelle) Further, it will be doubtless advisable to do some transition training. This applies to all the disciplines for which the athlete is preparing.

I planned my goals according to my dreams: I wanted to do Nice and Hawaii, then I wanted to take part in the Olympic Games! I am a donkey and I need a carrot. You have to set yourself a specific goal and not go off in all directions. I limit myself to two or three goals per season.

In 1986, when I went to Hawaii to see the Gods – Dave Scott, Mark Allen or Paula Newby Fraser – I would never have thought I would have a day like theirs. The idea took a long time to come to fruition from the moment I witnessed that race (it seemed unreal to me, unattainable), and the day I realised my dream, ten years later. It must have taken five years for me to accept the idea, even that it was finally do-able, and five more years to make the dream reality.

To get to the Olympics we knew that we had to go through the world cup. So we took part, with the intermediate goals of mastering the specific race conditions and getting to know our rivals in order to be ready for the ultimate goal, the Games.

(Béatrice) For the 1999 season my goals were the national grand prix (three races one after the other at the start of the season) and the world championships (in September). Between times, I concentrated on doing well in one or two ITU races for the points. You have to limit the number of goals and prepare for them specifically for a minimum of eight weeks (more for the long distances).

We haven't really formalised our career goals other than with regard to our competitive deadlines. However, it is true that in the course of a season we have looked for ways to include drafting among our goals by including certain cycle races in our timetable so as to be able to get used to changes of pace. Or by improving our running technique because running is now crucial in triathlon. So we have joined the Aix-les-Bains athletics club to specifically work on running during the winter period.

In fact, elite triathletes' preparation is more specific today and is approaching that of specialists in any of the three disciplines. Before, we could adopt an empirical or approximate approach. It's no longer the case today. Now triathletes train with 'real' cyclists, 'real' runners, 'real' swimmers. It's the same for all aspects formerly considered adjuncts in preparation (weight training, mental preparation, nutrition, stretching, medical back-up) which have taken on enormous importance.

(Isabelle) I prefer to work a month-and-a-half to two months on basic conditioning, with some threshold or maximum aerobic power work (if not I easily get dozy) and concentrate a lot on technique, with strengthening work on specific muscle groups.

From mid-February onwards or the beginning of March the pre-competitive season starts, during which maximum aerobic power work is more frequent, threshold work is maintained, as well as a long session in each discipline, to which are added specific transition sessions. Today, however, we do far less transition work than in the past. Before we did quite tough combinations of cycling (track or home-trainer) and running, but it did us good.

April is either a sharpening or competitive period during which we favour short, intensive sessions, stretching, recovery, short combinations, and polish up the adaptations and adjustments to our equipment.

After the first series of competition, we have a week's break towards the end of June or the beginning of July, and attack a short cycle of three weeks of basic conditioning (so the base of this second pyramid is smaller than the first) followed by two to three weeks of pre-competitive work and ten days of peaking for the world championships deadline.

At a level of general physical and muscular preparation, although the bulk of the work is done from January to the end of March (15 days before the first competitions) we work on our toning throughout the whole year through PPG (general physical preparation, Author's note).

Presentation of a specific preparation cycle: Hawaii 1995

(Isabelle and Béatrice)

We started to prepare specifically for Hawaii two months before D-Day. Up until then we had done the first half of the season over the short distance, but at the same time including each week from the beginning of the season a long ride (more than 100km) as well as a long run (at least an hour-and-a-half) about every ten days.

We arrived in Hawaii 15 days before the race, and came down from altitude three weeks before D-day. The last week before the race was for storing up maximum energy, training being limited to six to seven hours during the week, mainly devoted to final adjustments. The last week but one we reduced our mileage by half, retaining a long bike ride and run at half the distance of the race, namely 90km and 21km. The week before had been a 'cool' week, insofar as we came down from altitude (and then there was the trip!). The stay at altitude obviously comprised the biggest block of work. It is in the course of this stay that we set our training record with an historic week of 37hr 30min. We were there at the same time as Rob Barel and we often trained with him. It rained and snowed, and we went for pre-breakfast jogs in the snow at 2000m altitude knowing we were preparing for Hawaii... As compensation, we spent 20 minutes in the sauna every evening in order to get used to the intense heat that was to come! At least, we were mentally prepared for it. In the course of these three weeks, the middle week was the busiest. The first four days were for acclimatisation, followed by ten very hard days, with bike rides of 150km to 160km including mountain passes, and long runs with track sessions of 3x3000m for example. In the weeks before this stage we progressively increased the loads in order to progress from our typical short distance training to training for Hawaii. We went, for example, for two runs a day (it's less traumatic than a single long run) the first before breakfast and the second in the evening, including intervals. The run on an empty stomach got us used to drawing on our fat reserves. After 30 minutes of running, in fact, you physiologically simulate the end of a marathon. From the outset, you dip into your fat reserves, which helps you to confront the famous 'wall' after two to three hours of effort.

When we prepared for the Olympics, we trained on average 25 hours a week (this volume of work drops naturally in a period of competition). The volume is less than what we used to do several years ago when we could withstand a heavier work load, closer to 30 hours a week. So the change (in 1995) to Ironman-type training has not been particularly troubling as far as loads are concerned. There were fewer sessions but they were longer.

Ideally, a novice should prepare a year in advance for his first triathlon. More than for the elite athlete, general physical preparation is very important in order to avoid all risk of injury. What is more, the novice should be supervised and should be able to benefit from technical advice which will allow him to 'swim easy' or not to pick up faults in running.

In terms of programming, the winter months should revolve around multi-sports and endurance training: mountain biking, walking, cross country skiing, etc. When spring arrives, long and slow work should be retained, as well as beginning short and specific work with more intense intervals. And from April on you have to include transition sessions. For example, getting off the bike and running 3km in order to feel the unusual sensation of the cycling-running transition, which will be the real shock of the first triathlon you do.

For a sporting novice (who can also swim!), eight weeks of specific, applied preparation is enough to finish a first Olympic-distance triathlon without wishing to be too ambitious.

We really think that you have to begin with some short distances and at least a middle distance race before launching yourself into a Hawaii-style event. In our opinion, two to three years practice is a necessary precondition to be ready to face a long distance race, above all an Ironman which can last 12 hours and more. It will certainly be necessary to come to terms with the problem of the distance and transition and also nutrition, which is crucial over the long distance, and something you have to get used to, and that is not so easy. How many athletes do not finish, simply because they did not know how to feed themselves or who had difficulties with digestion? Fundamentally, what differentiates the short and long distance is the mentality. The approach to training is totally different when you are preparing for a long distance event as opposed to the Olympic distance. The short distance specialist needs the outside world to express themselves at will, needs rivals, aggression, while the long distance specialist is a hermit, an autonomous athlete who should train alone so as to be mentally strong.

(Isabelle) I think men are able to go further physically than women, but the latter are stronger mentally. Besides, it has been shown that fewer women drop out of long distance events than men.

Karen Smyers

My first rule of preparation is to make sure that I am recovering between work-outs and from week to week. There is often a cumulative fatigue from doing hard training, and if you don't allow your body to recover and bounce back, if you fit in too much intensity because you are trying to do three sports, your performance starts to deteriorate rather than improve. Therefore I am constantly monitoring my body signals.

There is a necessity to take a long-term approach in order to not over-race, not neglecting a good base before doing too many intervals.

You need to pay attention to your nutrition, to make sure that you are not depleting your body by putting too much stress on it. Check that you have enough vitamins and minerals, that you are adequately hydrated after work-outs, etc.

Taking part in recreational races requires five to seven hours a week, five to seven work-outs: one every day, or one on Monday, Wednesday, Friday and two consecutive sports during the week-end. Bike-run on Saturday, and swim-bike on Sunday.

In general people think you have to do a lot more than what you need to do. The biggest problem is that you have to do the entire swim without sinking to the bottom of the pool or of the lake, while if you are tired on the bike you can coast, and walk during the 'run'.

To prepare for the Olympic distance, though the global weekly average might be the same, it might take more weeks to build up for an Olympic race. Maybe ten to 12 weeks instead of six weeks.

For an Ironman, the minimum to be a finisher would probably be one hour a day until the weekend and four to five hours a day during the weekend. Meaning around 13 to 14 hours a week.

Goals may range anywhere from completing a certain distance race to improving each segment within the triathlon to improving your times on a particular course year after year, to comparing yourself to other people in your age group or division.

A good goal should be measurable, be dependent upon elements that you control. I generally recommend that people do not choose more than two major goals. You could have some short-term, intermediate goals along the season. It is hard to really peak more than twice during that April-to-November triathlon period.

A typical season: My preparation begins with a down period in December and January with aerobic activity only, to mentally and physically rejuvenate. During this period I continue to swim, bike and run. In February, I start bumping up the swim and run mileage without adding to my intensity. I do most biking indoors, using intervals. In March, the big focus is on base mileage: outside biking, more intensity running, and getting consistency in the pool. In April, my priority is more intensity while keeping the mileage fairly high. My first race is usually pencilled in for the end of April.

The rest of the season depends on my targets: if I have planned Nice at the end of June, for example, I keep both mileage and intensity high until one or two weeks before the race, then I taper off. (Tapering will, of course, be longer for an Ironman than for a Nice distance). After that race, I take one or two weeks of recovery, and then start a new cycle. I focus on shorter races in July and August: during that period I do a lot of speed work and sharpening.

Eight weeks prior to Hawaii, I start a six-week build-up programme where I increase my long runs week to week and I add intensity to the bike rides. I use one week to race in the middle of this period so that I don't lose too much of my speed. Then I have a long taper for two weeks.

I continue with a couple of short races afterwards, after two to three weeks of complete recovery, with a lot of massage and swimming. I do not run for seven to eight days at all then start with short runs afterwards which never last more than 40 minutes.

Weekly profile (short distance): In short-distance preparation a typical week would look like this: running, four to five runs a week, five hours altogether, ranging from a 30min recovery run to a typical 1hour 30min long run; biking: six sessions per week, averaging two hours, from a one hour recovery ride to 3 to 3hrs 30min; swim: five sessions of an hour each. Altogether, a total of 20 to 25 hours per week.

For long distance training, the structure of the week changes and the week-end becomes the focus of the week with a 100-mile ride or five hours on Saturday, and a long run on Sunday from 1hour 30min to 2hr 15min for my longest run (I add on ten to 15 minutes per week until I get to about 2hr 15min). After that, I need one or two recovery days for my legs, like an easy recovery bike ride, no hard gears. But during these days, I usually keep on swimming intervals, and usually on Wednesday I go for a five or six-hour straight training: I swim one hour (open water), I bike for three hours (I include some intensity work in it, and practice what I am going to drink and eat during the Ironman), and I run 1hr 30min, a very good way to teach me how to run through fatigue, how to swim straight for an hour. The only other speed I would do, would be on Friday (if I am feeling up to it) and I would consider some run intensity.

My training is not that much different during most of the season. I may do more base training at the beginning of the year, I might also perform longer bikes and runs, but my overall mileage has not changed that much.

I have had to cut back on the number of races I do, when I focus on the Ironman for six to eight weeks. I find it hard to race and do long distance training at the same time.

Lothar Leder

As a European you have to switch off in November (or October). I have taken off four complete weeks every year for ten years now. No sport, just three swimming sessions or three long runs, to let my muscles and whole body recover.

Hawaii has been the end of my season for years. Straight after the Ironman, I fly home (the next day), because I hate staying there after the event. Once I had a very bad race and unfortunately I had planned two weeks of vacation afterwards. I went nuts! So it is a safety issue for me: the race is always on Saturday, and I am out of Kona on Monday.

In December I start the build up very easy. I take it easy because Christmas is in sight and my real training will only seriously start at the beginning of January.

I have three months of base work then. You have to fly to the South of France, to Spain or to wherever the climate is warm to train properly.

You don't go crazy in the first three months, although it all depends in fact on what your goals for the season are. If I want to be fit very quickly, I start racing in April (cycle races and runs). If not, I start my triathlon season in May or June, it is easier.

When the weather gets warmer, you feel better and more positive mentally and it is easier to train faster and you get hot for racing.

In 1999 I planned my season differently: I stayed in Australia for six months, and this was the first year I had no break after Hawaii. That was a major mistake. I finished third in Hawaii and thought: yeah! I am superman! I can bang-bang-bang do anything. I was mentally very tough. I said to myself: ok, I won't have a break, I'll go on. I tried to maybe imitate Brad Beven in his old days, when he never had a break. I thought I could do the same. But I got the flu and was sick in January-February-March. I even took this tiredness into the European season. Your body needs to rest...

I have two long races a year: usually Roth and Hawaii. And I plan everything around these races.

I plan from race to race. I do not like to plan half-a-year ahead. My training programme goes three weeks in advance, not more, because you never know what is coming up, if you are going to be tired, sick or injured.

The year 2000 was really tricky, with the worlds in Perth in April ending the qualifying period for the Olympics, and the Sydney Games triathlon in September. So you had to peak twice in the year, and plan a real rest after the worlds if you wanted to be good in September... Everybody went crazy about it, beginning serious training very early in November. I decided to do the opposite and take it easy, as I do every year in the winter-time, until mid-March. I had to get fast really late (end of March beginning of April). I decided to pick maybe two of the world cups then, to get myself going and to qualify. Preparing for Sydney was a real problem for me also because my heart was with the Ironman... I even wanted to do a long distance race before Sydney... unless the federation kicked me out before! In fact, nothing went as planned and I failed to qualify for the Games. So what! I prepared like never for Roth and won it again!

To return to the general rules which guide my preparation, I never train if I do not want to, and I never run if I am tired. I always try to train with other people (70 percent of my training is in groups) so as not to get bored and get too slow, to remain always motivated and to have fun.

And I never do transitions (I never run after biking, for example). I figured out it makes me too tired, it is like a race for me. I did it in Australia during the winter in 1998/1999 when I trained with Col Stewart (one of the two best Australian coaches, Author's note): all three disciplines together and mixed up, in my preparation for short distance racing (I'd never do that for the long distance, although all triathletes preparing for a long course go running 20km after a bike ride).

For a promo race eight hours a week is enough: run three times 30 minutes, bike twice two hours and swim three times 30 to 45min. As for the Olympic distance, a maximum of ten hours seems more than enough.

And long distances? Fifteen hours per week, not 50. Fifty is Thomas Hellriegel. But that's a different story... I saw him training 56 hours when I was in the same room. And it is not about doping. I saw how he trains, it is crazy. He goes to bed at 8.30pm, wakes up at 10:00am... If we had a 200km bike ride, later in the day I'd go for a 10km run when he would come home after 20km. You always think you have done more than him, but he always does one hour more! It makes you crazy. He simply loves it.

So, 15 hours per week for long distance has to be enough. Because most people have to work, and triathlon is anti-social, it kills the family and your private life. In this perspective, you need one full year to prepare an Ironman, biking at the week-end, swimming consistently three times a week (although swimming is not important for beginners to prepare an Ironman), several running sessions including one long run consistently every week (20km), a bit longer (25km) as you approach race date. It is easy to bike long, but running is the most difficult part of an Ironman. This consistent long run is really an obligation so as not to pop during the marathon. This 1hr 45min-2hr training run boosts your confidence and helps you overcome the obstacle.

I define my goals with my dreams... and my sponsors. But what I want comes first. I am not a straightforward guy, I may change my mind in the middle of the season. In 1998 I had decided not to do Hawaii, but I like the race so I finally went. In 2000, being in excellent shape for the Olympic Games, it would have been easy to top out for Hawaii afterwards.

My goal is to make a living out of triathlon, to make money. This is the reason why I race a lot: normally two to three long distance races and 15 short ones. The number of races I do has increased because with drafting triathlon has become easier. I do some bike races but less every year, as I improve. When I was a junior I did a lot of racing, running (road and cross-country), biking (road races) and skiing. Now, as a pro, you just race-race-race, you don't have time for other types of racing. I often look back when I had a lot of fun racing other sports. But today, you cannot make money in a 10km run, because you get beaten by Africans, so you'd better go to a triathlon at the week-end!

As I said, we can have a maximum of two racing goals in a year. Then the main goal besides racing is to enjoy training. Triathlon is not about racing but about training. If you don't like training you won't enjoy racing.

So I have an 'off' cycle followed by a base training cycle. Then come race preparation cycles: they are always one or two weeks long. I plan from one day to the other until race day. After the race I shall have again a rest, and then I look for the next race.

I have a weekly cycle, but I train a lot on how I feel, I have a rhythm in between the races : I train, I get tired, I rest.

To prepare for long distance races, my cycle is six to eight weeks long. During the first four weeks (on the basis on an eight-week cycle), it is just mileage/hours consistently every week. And the last four weeks are the main part: I get really concentrated and I build up mileage until the last week which is taper. In other words, the highest mileage I reach is two weeks before the Ironman. But it is almost non-intensity. The year I went under the eight hours in Roth, I had reached 800km on the bike three weeks prior to race day and 1000km two weeks before. And the run then was 120km (down to 80km when tired from the bike). In terms of hours, this means 30 to 35 hours per week on average, with a maximum of 40. In the past I used to train more, but with age I have got a bit smarter and I train less: in the past I have done crazy things such as pushing up to 200km running a week in the first four-week period. Since I did not know how to train, I tried everything. Which gave me serious problems... This is another lesson to learn: in the last eight weeks leading to an Ironman, you should focus on never over-training, and never getting dehydrated. You do your Saturday evening 30km run, and suddenly you get dehydrated. It kills you for the next three weeks.

So I take a lot of care about dehydration now.

Regarding the run, I have trained in the past up to 150km a week leading to Hawaii... But in the last two years, I have run the fastest marathon splits in Hawaii, and I have never run more than 100km.

My body now has the experience of the past years. It is maybe Joanne King's secret: she has certainly done crazy things in the past, and now if she trains less she can be very fast. You have to do crazy things to be really good. Hellriegel apparently needed 56 hours to win Hawaii. He had terrible moments, when his immune system went down. Now he trains less and more efficiently. Experience...

With short distance racing, you get a kind of lazy mentality because you have to do less to keep your speed.

The exact opposite of Ironman preparation where you have to do more and more. So when you do not know what to do at night, if you should go for a run or not, preparing for a short distance you never go, preparing for Ironman you should go. This is difficult for me, because I am getting lazy anyway!

In terms of mileage, I train 15 to 20 hours a week for short distance racing, and 30 to 35 hours for Ironman.

When I'm preparing for the short distance, I have only one long ride (on Wednesday, 120km to 150km) and only one long run (25km, on Sunday) a week. I do these long training sessions because I think it is necessary for short racing, not because I have Roth or Hawaii in mind. You need to maintain an endurance base to be able to keep up the entire season of racing. For the rest, it is smart, fast swim training: not only swimmer's swim training, but triathlon swim training and transition training of course. I do butterfly for mental reasons, to feel powerful. And it is a good test: if you are able to swim a 50m or a 100m butterfly at the end of a training session, it means you are in a good shape.

In terms of mileage, my weekly average for short distance is 20km swim, 250km to 300km bike and 50km to 60km run.

I can switch from the short to the long like this: 'boom!' I have no problem, neither physically nor mentally. I am a big, strong guy. I have never been injured either in the Achilles or the knees, because I am full of muscles. That's not so good for running, but it helped me through the years. I did a lot of weight training when I was younger: as a junior, I did classical swim stuff like push-ups, butterfly machine, etc... (See Chapter Eight: Conditioning).

Luc Van Lierde

In my preparation, I concentrate more on swimming throughout the whole winter. I only give cycling and running priority when the good weather returns.

Concerning long distance, I do endurance during the winter and inject some intensity from the month of April onwards. For short distance the fast sessions should start from the month of January/February. In short distance, you should be able to withstand blood lactate levels of 10-11mmol/L while in long distance it rises to a maximum of 6mmol/L. In training, if there are no hard sessions, the lactate level falls away very quickly to values in the order of 4-5mmol/L and it is very difficult afterwards to make it rise. In fact, it takes several months. I rest a maximum of ten or so days each year. For example, after the European championships, I give myself a week of relative recovery, but in fact I rest only two days and start again the third day with half-an-hour of running or swimming. It's only when I'm travelling that I don't train. And in winter, there are two months during which I take a day off every fortnight or so.

In fact, the only time I really rest is at Christmas when I take a whole week. When you are young you can easily give yourself two to three weeks of rest without training at all. In contrast, the older you are the less you can give yourself this rest.

In general, I would say that you have to train a minimum that is equal to the time the race takes. Of course, everyone is different. But when you work eight hours a day and you don't have a sporting past, you can imagine that it might in the first place be necessary to concentrate on swimming. It is the most difficult discipline compared to cycling which should present no difficulty for beginners.

I know people who work who train more than me! In the morning before going to the office, at midday during lunch, and in the evening when they leave work. You need rest and free time. If you work full-time you should not train more than 15 hours a week.

Of course, if you want to do long distance your preparation needs to increase. I need three months of specific preparation before a long distance event, and I think that an average athlete should concentrate on this type of race about eight weeks beforehand. But this training should be preceded by steady training every day or every two days.

I am not alone in deciding my goals. I have sponsors who pay me and who have the same powers of decision over what races I should enter. I started triathlon for my own pleasure, but the day I finished third in the Belgian championships I decided to become national champion. Two or three years later my goal was to be the best in Europe. In 1995 I was second in the European championships. The following year I won and was second in the world championships. Over the years, the goals have become more and more ambitious. My best result up to now is to have won Hawaii. The only goal I have now is to become Olympic champion.

You can realistically have a maximum of three goals in a season. In fact, that depends on whether you are concentrating on the short or long distance. Nowadays, with drafting, you can be in form for three to five weeks, and for three to four times a year. Over long distance you can be in form for three races.

In 1999 I ran a lot of short distance races up to the European championships. After, I needed to do long distance training to get ready for Hawaii, and I needed a minimum of three months to be ready (Luc won Hawaii for the second time that year after finishing third in Nice, Author's note). That means it was impossible for me to do the short distance world championships.

In cycling I train with a group when I'm preparing for short distance racing, and alone for long distance. In running, I do much more track with a view to the short distance races. In general, the number of training sessions I do each week to prepare for the short triathlons (18) is more than when I train for the long (12 to 14). But of course, for two sessions of 60km in cycling for the short, I'll do one of 120km for the long.

For long distance you don't really need long sessions. They're only necessary for mental strength, to say that you have been on the bike for seven hours. My longest rides are over 200km when preparing for long distance, while 80km is enough for the short triathlon. In running, two sessions of 30 to 35km are enough before the Ironman, the last one about ten days before the event.

Philippe Martin

The first stage in the planning process is goal setting, a stage which is both crucial and a priority. To the extent in which it will be necessary to focus on and be ready for D-day, the programming needs to be very focused. The annual training programme is inferred from the goals. It is broken up into periods, each one aiming to contribute in part to reaching the goal or goals.

It is impossible to imagine a fixed, stereotypical programme because every athlete is unique. Nor can you have more than three goals each year. So, they might be the European or world championships, as well as a special event (Zofingen, Nice or Hawaii). Which, in my opinion, means that taking part in a circuit (European or world cup) makes the results very uncertain. Hence the need to pick the events on the circuit which suit the athlete and his needs best. For example, in 1998, our goal was the world championships in Lausanne (end of August, Author's note) and we opted for a simple periodisation beginning in January.

We work with mesocycles of four to six weeks with progressive increase in the loads for three weeks and relative recovery in the last week. The important competitions come at the end of the cycle when the whole training load is decreasing. Quality is maintained but the quantity drops significantly in this period of tapering. We try, however, to maintain speed work above the threshold (aerobic).

Six to eight hours a week should be enough for the novice to take part in his first triathlon. If he already knows how to swim, 80 percent of the time should be devoted to cycling/running, without any real priority (it depends on the wishes and relative talent of the athlete in each of the disciplines). There is no real difference between the distances for promo/sprint and the Olympic distance: it's strength of mind which will help the athlete through to the finish of the race in both cases.

As far as long distances are concerned, it seems to me that ten to 12 hours of weekly training (20 percent devoted to swimming and 40 percent to the other two disciplines) are enough to finish Nice without spending a week in intensive care.

If there is any specific training for the long distance that can be applied to the short, it is at the level of the amount of training. And again, that depends on the athlete: certain competitors who specialise in short distance really train too much!

To give an example, you could say that a cycle ride of five hours in the saddle is suitable for long distance while two hours is enough for the Olympic distance. In running, a session of up to three hours is recommendable to prepare for long distance, as opposed to one hour for the short. Above all, you have to concentrate on quality, and be capable of running the Olympic distance 10,000m in less than 30 minutes.

Simon Lessing

Each season should start with three to four months of base training, in all three disciplines, with no intensity. Just trying to improve your technique and do some strength work, too, where and when needed. During this period, bike rides will be longer but you never work at a high intensity. Without this base work it is very difficult to last through the entire triathlon season, since each year you virtually have 11 months of racing.

Then start working a little bit more on intensity when you start to race, working at your certain objective throughout the year, cutting down on distance, working a bit more on speed work and fartlek work-outs. This will bring you through and maintain a high level of fitness during the race season.

Many athletes do not do enough work in the winter; they have a good start to the season and then blow out after two months of racing. That is really because they don't have the base work behind them that they could have done in the winter period.

European athletes should never go to Australia in the winter period. It is a big mistake to start racing too soon. Through my own experience, I can only ask for six months of racing in a year. Anything more and I start to go downhill. Asking for nine to ten months of high competition racing is unrealistic and too much on the body. A lot of athletes, among them the Australians who race their season and then the European season (I am not going to give any names) would be much faster and more competitive if they had an active break sometime during the year.

It is important after your season to take a real break from the sport for six weeks. During this period I like to do a couple of runs a week or a couple of swims, just the basics to keep the level of fitness.

This is why I did not race the world championships in Wellington '94 (they took place in November; nor did he compete in Perth 2000 world championships in April, Author's note), having started in February already in Chile.

Going to Perth (the 1997 world championships were also in November)I knew it was going to be hard (Simon was only third that year, Author's note). I tried to delay my season by one month starting in March. But having said that, even if you don't race, you still have to train, and hard. However, I must say that sometimes not racing as much is even more tiring than training, because when you race you have to rest a bit before and a bit after.

I race 18 times a year on average.

To participate in a short distance triathlon at a reasonable level you need three to four work-outs per week in each discipline. But it really depends on your level of fitness, and your strengths and weaknesses in each discipline.

For a long distance triathlon you need four rides a week, with a long one (six to seven hours if you are preparing for an Ironman), the others being two hours. In running, four to five runs are necessary, including a long one every 14 days (meaning two hours, easy). In swimming four swims a week, with some longer stuff like three to four x1000m (one session a week) or 20x200m, meaning less speed and more endurance.

There are short and long term goals. Daily training, weekly race, the European or world championships, or a local race in your town.

For me, the most difficult part of the season is the winter time because you need to keep your motivation up while training for three to four months "for nothing".

Long-term goals for me would be the Olympic Games.

You need to be realistic in your goals, weighing the amount of training necessary and your strengths and weaknesses, otherwise you'll never satisfy them and you will feel very frustrated.

A maximum of three goals may be set, realistically I believe, in a season. They have to be set in order of priority. For example the European championships, the France Iron Tour and the world championships, with a good period between each where you can concentrate on those goals set in your training.

My overall training cycles are organised like this: a first cycle of three to four months of base training. Race cycles are then organised around the main goals. The very specific work should start two months before your goals. Only experience helps you understand what works for you.

My rule is to get so many work-outs in per week. I am not the type of athlete who says: every Tuesday I have to do a track work-out, every Wednesday a swim interval… I am able to adapt to the way I feel. We must listen to our body before anything else. Generally speaking, as long as I get the work-outs done, meaning five to six sessions a week in swimming, biking and running (each), with one hard (speed work stuff) session per week in running, two in swimming and one on the bike, races included, I am happy. I don't have specific set days, but my only rule is to have 48-hours rest between each hard set, no matter which sport.

I think there is absolutely no general rule comparable to other sports like, for example, the sprints in athletics.

When I was training for Nice, I actually did not modify my training, I simply added longer endurance work-outs: every ten days a two-hour run, two long rides (four hours) on Monday and Friday (or week-end, depending on how my week went), and one longer swim. Nice is not an Ironman, it only lasts six hours. And even for short distance triathlon training, you still have to train three to four hours a day.

Eduardo No Sanchez

First you need to know the dates of the important sporting events of the season, then you have to identify the goals with the elite athletes and put forward a budget to the federation for these goals! Then only is it possible to speak of planning, cycles and sessions.

These cycles and sessions are different for each athlete according to his age, his sporting background, his triathlon history, his level, etc. In short, each athlete needs a specific programme.

In terms of career, my priority with each athlete is to work on improving one discipline each year or each season (a year can have two seasons). For example, improving swimming strength.

In so far as we do not have a limitless supply of athletes, our priority is to avoid injury while including all forms of activity in the programme. There is a lot of recovery, reduced transition technique, cessation of training as soon as the slightest pain appears, and gentle distance work in running.

(See also the section on Work Cycles)

I think that five hours a week and two more Saturday and Sunday are enough to prepare a debutant for his first Olympic distance triathlon. Even less is needed to finish a promotion triathlon.

I finished Nice and Roth (4km, 120km, 30km, and 3.8km, 180km, 42km respectively, Author's note) with only about ten hours of training a week. But I did have a solid sports background. A non-sporting debutant won't finish a triathlon like this in good condition without long preparation and more quantity.

A goal is a very personal thing and not something that can be imposed from outside. There are different levels of objectives in triathlon. These might be obtaining certain results in a given competition (and these results have a different significance depending on whether you take part in the national championships or the world cup, the national championships or the European championships, the national championships or a regional event). On a different level these goals might concern physiological, psychological, technical or tactical aspects. But whatever the goals, what counts is their relation to the aptitude of the athlete, their training, their recovery and their general attitude as professional triathletes.

It is not realistic to have more than two competition goals per year. In contrast, several technical, tactical and psychological goals can be fulfilled each year and in the course of a career.

The programmes that I suggest to my athletes largely contain the following structure: two to three weeks development, one week recovery. That said, this rule depends on the time of year. In fact, the work cycles are longer and the rest cycles shorter in winter than in the competition phase.

In the same way, in the course of the week, two to three days of development alternate with one day of recovery and another two to three days of development.

Spaniards are traditionally very good runners. That's why I only timetable three days of running each week (volume: 30 to 50km, depending on the runners). In contrast, swimming takes place seven days out of seven, one or two sessions daily (volume: 20km to 35km depending on the swimmers). Cycling depends on the time of year, but the cyclists ride on average 250km a week. Strength training appears in general two or three times a week on my schedules.

I am not sure that specific training is necessary for long distances as opposed to the short. Mental strength, concentration, inner balance, hydration and nutrition seem to me more important factors than changing the training mileage in order to prepare for a long distance triathlon.

Susanne Nielsen

I don't have a general rule governing my training programme, apart from the fact that I force myself to do a certain amount of intensive training for two weeks. That way, if I'm not ready for a difficult session on a particular day, I can always postpone it to the day after. So 14 days is my reference point as a unit of intensity, even if my work cycles can last three to four weeks according to the time of year or the fact that I may be at training camp, for example.

Today, thanks to my long years of training, I can give more time to quality/intensive work and proportionally less to quantity. Because less energy goes on volume, I can invest more time in hard sessions, because I've got more time for them and more time to recover.

I see no difference in promo, sprint and Olympic triathlons, at least where beginners are concerned. Two to three sessions per discipline each week seem more than enough to me, but without intensity because intensive work does not seem appropriate for beginners.

After trying to persuade the debutant who had the preposterous idea of entering a long triathlon (in my opinion it's an act of folly to want to take part in a long distance triathlon without a decent sporting background!), ten hours a week seems necessary to me to comfortably prepare for a long distance triathlon like Nice. With a breakdown of six hours cycling and two hours of swimming and running. In running, it is important that the neo-triathlete should be able to run for 40 to 45 minutes at a steady pace and not too gently.

Never set yourself a goal that is unrealistic. Then, and only then, can you set yourself any goals! I personally aim for one goal for each race. It is not necessarily a question of winning, but, for example, of having two excellent transitions, or any other objective that allows me to gain in experience for the main goals of the season. In terms of results, I've always set myself a maximum of two to three goals each season, like the European and world championships, the qualification for Hawaii and Hawaii, to which I add my favourite race, for example.

My coach thinks it is absurd to double my mileage so as to be effective over long distances. At the present time, my longest weeks are 28 hours but I never do less than 20 hours a week.

Laurent Chopin

The key word in training is assimilating! You can do the best training in the world, but if it is not understood, it is, strictly speaking, worth nothing.

It is, on the other hand, worth taking into account three essential factors: the progression factor (training should let the athlete progress and increase his initial functional level); the reproduction factor (training should reproduce the situation and conditions of competition, so that the athlete is not lost on the day of the race); the balance factor (training should challenge to the least possible extent the extra-sporting environment of the athlete).

How much training? This question cannot be answered without considering, on a case by case basis, the athletes the training is for. What is their sporting background, what are their psychological and physiological qualities, what is their availability?

In any case, the idea that the amount of training should be proportional to the competition distance seems to me completely wrong. It's better this way! It is better to modify the content of the sessions, to adapt them to the specific effort required for long distance.

Training is not an exact science. I have seen triathletes finish the Embrun Ironman on a derisory training load considering the difficulty of this course. Other parameters, more or less quantifiable than the amount of training, come into play, among them the degree of motivation.

Having taken all these precautions, let's try to reply now to this tricky question!

Let us depart from the principle that the desired goal should be based on the following competitive practice, of not suffering too much, of not finishing too extravagantly, and of wanting to compete again just afterwards.

Eight to 12 weeks of preparation at a rate of four to five weekly sessions (about five hours) should suffice to prepare for a promo, divided up – although it depends on the athlete's background – in the following way:

Swimming: two sessions of one hour, with the emphasis on physiological technical development.

Cycling: one session for developing aerobic qualities (basic endurance), learning specific skills (gears, balance, direction, etc).

Running: recovery jogging followed by five to ten straight sprints.

Multi-transitions: the specific session of the week, touching on the essence of the triathlon (systematic function) on a base of development of physiological qualities (either in cycling, running or both).

For short distance, the same eight to 12 weeks of preparation, this time based on five to seven sessions a week (about eight to 12 hours) divided up as follows: two swimming sessions – one or two cycling sessions – two running sessions – one session of multi-transitions. The programme detail follows the same model as above, adding a session developing physiological qualities in cycling or running.

Long distance is an entirely different problem because psychological factors play a large part compared to promo or short distance. Experience counts enormously. The ability to distribute your effort equally: pace management in competition is essential in order to experience, in a positive manner, a long triathlon.

It requires more time learning in training. Finally, you need to manage your nutrition during the race.

Before taking part in your first long distance race, I would recommend putting one or two seasons behind you, in order to lay the foundations of physical conditioning, all of which is included in the logic of progression mentioned above.

But once again, just because the individual concerned wants to take part in a long triathlon does not mean that his volume of training should be increased tenfold! If his timetable does not let him train more than eight to 12 hours, the gates of long distance are not necessarily closed to him.

For example, Xavier Galea (double world long distance champion with the French team) does no more training, in terms of number of hours, than my athletes specialising in short distance. Only the content of the sessions, the work rate and the times vary.

More concretely, in a 12-hour cycling week, the athlete training for the short distance will do, for instance, two sessions (one of pure maximum aerobic power and one mixed of maximum aerobic power/race pace) and the rest basic endurance; for long distance, the specific session will be carried out over longer distance intervals at lesser intensity and I will add a long session for basic endurance.

In running, basic runs will increase a little in length, one long run (never exceeding 90-120 minutes) will be programmed and the interval session will evolve on the same model as the one set out for cycling.

I use transitions to create conditions of pre-fatigue in cycling allowing me to move directly to a certain pace in running. The advantage is obvious: it lets you simulate a long session while limiting the extreme running effort.

It is becoming more and more difficult to include preparation for a long distance triathlon during a season centred on the short. That said, it is clear that the winter period can be exploited to develop aerobic qualities which would allow ten to 12 weeks of specific long work to be programmed in and have a good race. The short distance triathlons in this terminal period would act as no more than special sessions, staging posts en route to the long distance goal.

An athlete's goals depend above all on their intrinsic qualities, their desires and motivation. There are many types of goals, but for me there is one that is unavoidable: to find through the triathlon a beneficial balance for the athlete concerned between their sporting life and life outside sport. In other words, it would be impossible for me to coach an athlete with the one and only goal to make him a better competitor.

In terms of race-goals, it seems to me that three, maybe four are quite feasible in a short distance season (only two for long distance) with this basic structure: preparation, sharpening, post-objective recovery.

In outline, I divide the season into three cycles: two big and one small! The big cycles correspond to the periods of preparation (November-April) and competition (May-September) the small is for rest and recovery (October).

Classically (and a little out-of-date), you can think of a triathlete training in the water like a swimmer, on a bike like a cyclist and running like a runner. The athlete is only a triathlete on the day of competition. Personally, I think that you have to train the triathlete like a triathlete during the whole preparation period, with certain triathlon-specific sessions in the three disciplines, and that he should be, on the day of the triathlon, a swimmer, cyclist and runner. In other words, I try to see to it that the triathlete performs in the three sections of the triathlon as closely as possible to his optimum level in each of the three disciplines that he has practised separately.

Preparation period (short distance, November to April)

Swimming:

(November-December) Technical work. The four styles. Return of sensation. Flow work. Controlling breathing. Short reps. Reduced mileage, but increasing progressively until the end of December. Waterpolo for fun, cohesion and group management, for something different from normal, but also to bring back the taste for speed.

(January-March) Base work. Increase of mileage. A lot of aerobic work. Triathlon-specific development: start sessions, changes of pace. Technique maintenance.

(April) Swimmer-type development. Global reduction in mileage, while retaining the long aerobic sessions. Development of base speed.

Cycling:

(November-15 December) Recovery. Mountain bike trips. Reduced mileage. Technical work. Small gears.

(15 December-February) Progressive increase in global mileage and bike-mileage. A lot of aerobic work. Four to five weeks at pace. Pedal cadence. Five to six weeks of threshold development. Weight training.

(March-April) Progressive reduction in mileage, retaining a wide aerobic base. Development of maximum aerobic power. Specific race development. Mixed sessions of speed-maximum aerobic power.

Running:

(November-February) Jogging. Long runs, increasing progressively (from one hour to one hour 40min). Preparation of race physique. Technical work. Improvement of maximum aerobic speed.

(March-April) Jogging. No more long runs. Threshold development. Race-specific development: mixed speed/maximum aerobic speed sessions.

To stick to the specifics of the triathlon, the cycle/run transitions are done almost systematically during this period. Sometimes, it may only consist of ten 100m strides coming off the bike.

The programmed sessions are thought out in terms of length and not in terms of which discipline is practised. For example, if the aerobic ride on Sunday morning with the club is two hours 30 minutes, it is no longer for me the Sunday morning ride, but will be broken up into two hours ten minutes on the bike and 20 minutes running.

Transitions of this type will vary, both in form and length, in the course of the preparation phase and according to the type of objective-type development. I can, for example, combine a session of specific bike development with a specific running development session.

I also use multi-transitions very early on in the preparation phase and not only in the running development phase. I do this respecting the work steps outlined above with regard to the type of physiological goal pursued.

Competition period (short distance, May to September)

This period is difficult to manage because it has to match the outline of each athlete's goals. You have to be particularly careful that the combination of competitions does not lead to either a progressive loss of form or to over-training. The loss of form will be caused by a succession of triathlons which will not allow, apart from the pre-competition rest and the recovery that follows it, the athlete to maintain the functional level achieved at the beginning of the competition phase. Over-training will be brought on by insufficient recovery between races.

Thus, if the timetable allows for it, it will be desirable in the middle of the season to interrupt the rhythm of competition and to redo the base work cycle, in order to start again from a healthy base in the second part of the season.

The programming of this period is seen, accordingly, as more delicate to manage because triathletes do not all react the same to the same race, both from a physical and psychological point of view. So it is necessary, at this moment more than ever, to take into account the characteristics of each individual.

It is for all these reasons that it is impossible to give a programme-model of this period.

Rest and recovery (October)

Rest is necessary for the physical and psychological regeneration of the athlete. Two weeks of complete rest do not seem to me to be an aberration, or two weeks in which the athlete does one or two sessions of his choice (swimming, cycling, running, or a completely different sport). Two weeks will follow of re-acquaintance with the sensation of swimming and running with maybe a short mountain bike ride, all of this being carried out without any significant psychological pressure.

The figures, to finish…

My athletes' volume of work varies depending on the time of year, the goals pursued and the athletes' own qualities. But I look to favour a certain amount of consistency in training volume (weekly average from January to October: 18-19 hours).

So, sport by sport, the training averages from January to December rise in this way: 800 to 850km in swimming, 12,500 to 13,000km cycling, and 1,900 to 2,000km running.

CHAPTER FIVE

EVALUATION: THE TESTS

The notion (of evaluation) mingles the quantitative and the qualitative; the real and the ideal; ethics and the world of desire. Charles Hadji*

Why on earth evaluate?

Evaluate… the better to identify, understand, correct, act; the better to plan, organise, improve and attain the heights. Evaluate – because without feedback, without a return on the investment there is no chance of knowing if one is on the right path to the motorway or the garage. Evaluate – above all not solely for the sake of evaluation! Athletes and coaches do not have the time to waste with tests and procedures that lead to nothing concrete.

When to evaluate?

Before, during, after competition and training. Permanently, in the end. It's incredibly engrossing when you have to swim, cycle, run as well as eating and sleeping! It's very restricting when the urgency of the terrain demands that you act on the content of training, session after session, day after day…

Evaluate… but with what tools?

To evaluate well is to choose a good test, the appropriate equipment, the ideal place, the best distance, in order to observe without error, to identify without meeting any opposition, to correct without hesitation so that the subsequent performance is of the best.

This is the paradox of evaluation, the essential and unavoidable moment of every apprenticeship, of every education, of every research into perfection. Without it there is no progress possible. With it, so many questions, torments, anxieties, time spent and sometimes wasted?!

The athletes plunge into the water to express their certainties and their choices, their questions, their fatigue, faced with the tests whether they are in a laboratory or outside. They take up a position from the height of their whole experience so that we can see more clearly how to test their performance (in training and competition) in triathlon…

Brett Sutton

My personal opinion? Evaluation is unavoidable in every training session and each day gives rise to a particular evaluation.

I had an argument with my squad scientist once. The quotation I put to him was that every day for five hours for the last 20 years I was doing research. This is something I wanted to make very clear to him, because he was talking about tests and so forth, and I said every day I had to research that athlete, because every day he was going to be different to the next day. A coach who is a good judge will help an athlete. Some day, in this particular cycle, we have to say: he does not look good, we have to change. And this is one thing I find difficult with the said structure: it postulates that the people we are educating do not change. This is the structure. Boom! Today is the rest. Boom! Today is this. Boom! You can't do that, because at some stage you are going to either break down your athlete, because they are not particularly either psychologically or physically ready to do a particular programme. I watch their warm-up. If somebody is doing something particularly different (all of a sudden someone is doing a little stretching that he usually does not do), he is giving you a signal that he is not really tuned up for today. So I walk over and say: "Jeeezzz Greg, you look like you needn't do this today". He says: "oh no, we are going to do this track session!" And I say: "no session today". The guy was giving me signals he did not want to do it. He'd say yes, I want to do it, because he's got a brain. I used to train horses and dogs. They don't talk to you. You have to look and see what they are saying. So this athlete was thinking: I do not want to really do this, but I am going to do it because I have an ability to push myself through a period of time...

Athletes read paper differently. You can give the same programme to two athletes, and they will do two different programmes. So that's the first part of evaluation.

I no longer encourage my athletes to take part in laboratory tests for psychological reasons. However, sometimes, we do lab testing: VO_2max on the treadmill with the top athletes. Once again, I pick which athletes want to do it. Those who want to do it, do it, those who don't, don't do it.

In swimming, bio-mechanically we video them. And individually rather than as a group, we show them their strokes, because it is a little bit of a scary thing when some of them think they swim nice and they swim technically very poorly. So once again, I am always trying to protect the mentality, the psychology. It is very important. With swimming, we would also take the heart rate. We do 7x200m. Our lactate testing is done straight after. I test them once a month.

In running, I tend to work on aerobic tests, I will get them to run at a certain heart rate, and we would hope to see an improvement from test to test. We'll run 5km at 150, or 160 heart rate for certain athletes. And if they are running slower than the previous time, the training needs to be adjusted. And if they are running faster, obviously it is working. 3km is too short, it is too anaerobic. 10km would even be better, but then it becomes a training situation, so 5km (15 to 20min) is what I am looking for.

Testing bricks is an interesting concept, which I have to think about. I don't really need to worry about it too much, because I have done more brick work than anybody else on the planet at the moment. But this is a good point: I have never sat down and thought about that. I don't want to be evasive, I have done a lot in this area, but I haven't got it under control at all at the moment.

I'll tell you what I have been doing: I have been using a wind-trainer with a Wattometer, and what we have been doing is working under a certain amount of watts and then getting off and running at a certain aerobic heart rate. I can push harder and see how they are running, or I can give less watts. I want to find out if they are running more efficiently after biking with bigger gears or with no gear. In a draft situation, you can run a hell lot better than if you were riding on your own. What I would like to be able to do is develop the athlete's ability to finish the time trial and still be able to run as fast as they can do otherwise.

If an athlete doesn't have a running background but has a straight triathlon background, I think he runs faster after the bike than he would do in track races. Ben Bright is a good example: he did several road races where he was so slow that it scared me. We decided then to have him ride for an hour just before racing... and he ran very similar to the times that he is running races. So I think there is a motor skill pattern, that a triathlete is a triathlete, he has got the feel of getting off the bike and running, where they don't have the feel for the run. It is the same with Jackie Gallagher, who has no problem jumping off the bike and running superb times. Another good point too is that there are triathletes who are trying to be duathletes. Some people say: "These guys should be great duathletes". But they are not, because they are just not used to running first. This is a valid thing to look for in athletes.

I do not believe heart rate monitors should be allowed in races (laughs!). Our sport is being over-run. We've got to go back to the spirit of sport, and heart rate monitors are not part of it. They can be very tricky. I love having athletes with heart rate monitors racing with my athletes . I think they are at a disadvantage. Because sometimes things don't go the way they want them to go. Sometimes somebody has got to have a surge and you're going to say: "oh, my heart rate! I'd better not do that". What a disadvantage!

From a training point of view, the use of heart rate monitors in running, depending on the athlete, is 70 to 80 percent of the total. I would dictate their running programme from the heart rate, we are trying to achieve. So I think that as a working tool they are excellent.

On the bike, I find that we do a lot more work at a bigger gear than in Europe, so our heart rates are much slower on the bike. And I purposely do that. We don't care too much about the bike. My athletes will put their heart rate monitor when cycling, and they will be at a 130 to 140 heart rate. Why I do that is because I believe it keeps the system under control, and it strengthens their legs.

I don't think athletes should be wearing their heart rate monitor at long distance either. That's the human body against the elements. People who train themselves without a heart rate monitor tend to have a better feel for what they are doing. Because they are running on what they believe.

One other thing I found with my athletes (and I said I use the heart rate monitor all the time) is that they lose the feel of the tempo because they are worrying about this. Some day they can be feeling very down, although they are running biomechanically very well. They look at their heart rate monitor and say: "Hooo, my heart rate is terrible". Another day their heart rate is great but their legs are trash, because they did a big bike session. So what do we believe? Do we just throw it all out?

A much better solution would be to have them wear their heart rate monitors, but not see the heart rate. It is like timing. One of the problems with races, and with training, is that the athletes always want their time. You cannot put them on a track... I make them take their watches off. If you learn to control them in that area, they'll do much better workouts. In fact, I'm less and less interested in timing a certain distance (subject to variations and according to the other disciplines practised) and more in consistency of a series. Thus, the time for a 400-metre freestyle no longer interests me today, I prefer the average over 20x100m which seems to me much more representative of the shape they're in as long as they don't focus on the sacrosanct stopwatch.

Finally, that is the hard question when you talk heart rate monitors to me: They are good and bad at the same time.

Grégoire Millet

It is necessary to test when training starts again to readdress the training phases. With young people, it is also useful to follow their progress and keep track of how their performances develop. Finally, testing is necessary from the moment that certain indicators (technical, for example) start to flash.

Running-cycling-running transition in the laboratory. Ideally, this test should be carried out when training starts again (November-December), just before the first competitions (April) and in the middle of the season (end of July-August). Unfortunately, for practical or human reasons, I've always had to make do with the first two tests. The cycling part is done on an Orion ergo-cycle, the running on a treadmill. This test, developed together with the laboratory of sport sciences at Besançon, consists of seven minutes running at the average speed of the 10km triathlon run. It is followed by a test for maximum aerobic power in stages of three minutes then two minutes cycling, followed by a steady period (cycling) at 80 percent of the maximum aerobic power achieved. Finally, once again, there is seven minutes running at the same pace as the first effort. That helps evaluate maximum aerobic power and to reach an estimate of: the thresholds with ventilatory parameters in cycling, energy expenditure at a specific speed in running, the degradation of this energy expenditure under the influence of an exhausting test in cycling, and finally, thanks to the use of a kinematic arm, mechanical expenditure.

In running, for a long time I tested maximum aerobic speed of my athletes using Léger-Boucher or Brue-type tests. Nowadays, I have done away with these because I can estimate maximum aerobic speed using a simple 6x1000m rep session, for example.

It's the same in swimming where I use series-tests, like 15x100m at an average 1500m speed with intervals of one minute 30 seconds to see where my athletes are. I can just as easily use more recovery in this series or get them to do 6x200m with a sufficiently long recovery to be able to estimate lactate levels with an Accusport.

I was one of the first to use a heart rate monitor in training. All my athletes have them together with a computer to check their heart rate profiles when they want.

The interest in the heart rate monitor is multiple: stabilising effort, comparison of recovery profiles, change in pulse, etc.

I make use of pace charts for control when I'm doing progressive work. For example, in a session of 200, 400, 600, 800, 1000m in running, where the 1000m should be covered in three minutes ten seconds, at the end of a series where the 200m would be run at two minute 50 second pace.

Isabelle and Béatrice Mouthon

(Isabelle) There is no need to evaluate training because this evaluation is in any case incomplete. It mainly takes into account physical qualities and is found extremely wanting with regard to the crucial influence that mentality has on performance. So it can be seen that the people who are competitive in training are not necessarily so in competition. To the extent that the qualities which are tested in training do not always reveal the qualities that the athlete shows in competition, the latter is in fact the only true means of testing.

There are laboratory tests but also numerous points of reference in training which can lead to an evaluation. But to test without references is difficult, only the comparison of test results and the performances of an athlete from year to year makes sense.

(Béatrice) I completely agree with Isa. That said, it is always preferable to rely on even incomplete tests when there is no other reference point. So, in endurance sports, when you mention testing you think immediately of VO_2max tests, which are interesting indicators for the athlete. In the same way, tests at a sports medical centre or the simple pulse check at rest or after 1000m on the track is worthwhile information.

(Isabelle) For me evaluation only has a point at the end of a chain of events, when you come out of a process of training aimed at reaching certain specific objectives and when you are at the peak of your powers which have been developed during a certain amount of time.

We fill in, of course, our training logs which we consider a training assessment but not an evaluation.

In the same way, we use "evaluative" sessions and tests, not for evaluation in the strict sense, but as a means of planning our sessions and getting our bearings.

(Béatrice) For me testing is a point of reference, it's a point of departure for training. What is more, you have to bear in mind that this reference point is only useful for a very, very short time...

(Isabelle and Béatrice) We have always been tested in the sports medical centre, most notably the famous objective VO_2max test on the bike, even when we were doing swimming. When we became triathletes we did more specific tests under the guidance of Grégoire Millet who has created his own test. His aim was to evaluate the deterioration in technique and energy expenditure during a double transition running/cycling/running (for the details see the comments of Grégoire Millet in this same chapter, Author's note) We have not done any other test in the laboratory with Grégoire.

Our more recent collaboration with Patrick Dreano has led us to more specific VO_2max tests for cycling and running. Moreover, we have two specific tests in cycling: one that aims to estimate maximum power output, the other testing our top speed at maximum pedalling frequency. These tests are carried out in November and April.

Patrick has a swimming test consisting of 8x50m with 30 sec recovery between each interval, at maximum pace and trying to be as consistent as possible. We did it once. In fact, to the extent that we are independent in our training (we do not depend on any national centre in particular) it is difficult for us to respect any testing system, because we are never in the right place at the right time. We have our reference points, the times that we do running, for example, over six to 10x400m with 1min to 1min 20sec recovery, or 4 to 5x1000m with three minutes recovery.

In cycling, we don't have a standard course. The only comparisons that we can make are the way we feel when we climb a hill near us.

In swimming, our reference is a session of 10x100m with an interval of 1min 30sec in order to gauge pace, average time and recovery.

This whole battery of tests quantifies (objectively) the form we are in. But on a daily basis it's feeling that is most useful, ease of effort, and the ability to recover that serve as a point of reference. Session after session, day after day, feeling provides a subjective self-evaluation of form.

We've been using a heart rate monitor for seven years but use it less and less nowadays and only for certain sessions.

(Isabelle) Patrick Dreano's work uses the heart rate monitor a lot in order to set out the sessions, especially at the start of the season. In fact, I like to use it when I'm tired to see where I am and so that I don't push myself too much (although, in fact, we know ourselves very well and we no longer really need it).

(Béatrice) I prefer to work with sensations (breathing rhythm), but I love to have a control device when I'm working on a specific cycling or running session, simply because if I have no difficulty surpassing myself in competition I find it difficult to push myself when training.

Patrick Dreano's training is based on steps and the use of charts which he works out at the start of the year after evaluation tests. So, to be able to follow his training, we have to wear heart rate monitors the whole time. In fact, we think we know ourselves well enough not to have to have recourse to them. Moreover, heart rate develops rapidly with the level of training, which makes the charts change.

Heart rate in fact defines the pace (stopwatch) that we should go at in swimming, cycling and running.

Karen Smyers

I test myself almost daily! I lay out my programme for the week, but I may discover on Tuesday that I am not going to do it, depending on how I recover from work-out to work-out, on my mental disposition (if I am getting in a bad mood, which is often a sign of over-training). You have to learn to distinguish between not feeling like training because you are being lazy and not feeling like training because you are truly over-trained. And only experience tells what true tiredness is.

Surprising as this may seem, I've never really had the opportunity to have access to lab testing, etc.. Of course, I have had the occasion sporadically in the past to have my VO_2max tested once a year. But my values have not really developed this last seven to eight years. In contrast my threshold levels have changed upwards.

I test myself more by seeing how I am when I wake up in the morning. But it is hard for me to know beforehand if it is going to be a hard day. I need to go there, to warm up, try the first interval then I might feel actually quite good. I generally do not have trouble motivating myself to push hard if I am up to it. If my times are off, it is generally physical and not mental.

Swim-bike-run tests? I don't do any tests to find out what my transitions are like. I just compare my times from week to week, year to year. In swimming, a set of 4x500yards (about 450m, Author's note); in cycling, a 10-mile time trial (about 16km, Author's note), the same rolling hills bike course; running, 3x1 mile (about 1600m, Author's note) or 6x800m.

Right now I am using the heart rate monitor in training, more as a tool to learn about what I do, rather than to dictate what I do.

Lothar Leder

Testing is a permanent process. Day and night. You sometimes get tired of it, but it is necessary.

When I was younger, I followed the German Federation testing programme, every three months. Now I have my own tests. I hate being tested in swimming because I am not a good swimmer and it is really hard for me to improve.

In running I have a two kilometre loop in the woods. On the bike, I do always the same loops: I have a lovely 60 km loop, a 100 km loop, a 160 km loop and a 200 km loop.

I know my times (everything is written down).

So before the world championships, for example, I try to beat my best running time over the two kilometre loop: it is downhill. Sounds like cheating (I hate testing!) because my times are extremely fast, but it works for me, it makes me feel good. And if I have a tail wind on the bike, it is even better: I push harder!

I was really talented when I was young. After my lab tests (when I was 17), they told me: you are going to win Hawaii. Then you get too big-headed, you think you are good. It is not good when you think you are good. You are never good enough.

I stopped lab testing long ago because it was too difficult for me. I was doing it in East Germany, so I had a six-hour car drive to the place, four times in a year; furthermore, we had to be always in the same testing conditions (you know, in the last three days preceding a test, you had to taper). And all your training was based on the results at the tests. Too much for me. The main reason why I stopped is that I was losing a full week: one day travel, two days tests, one day travel...

The only moment when I tested my transitions was in Australia in 1999 with Col Stewart (together with Brett Sutton considered the best Australian coach. Col is the father of Miles, the 1991 world champion and the first Australian in the Sydney Games, Author's note).

Ah! Heart rate monitors...I used them in the old days. It is very good if you are on your own. For example you put in 160 or 170 for the beep. If I were too slow, it'd start to beep, so I was forced to run fast. I used it for a few years, and then I stopped... Battery got empty, always! So I am not using heart rate monitors anymore. But I am not saying they are not good. If I had a coach and my coach asks me to wear one, I'd do it. But I have no coach and I am too lazy.

Luc Van Lierde

I test my lactate level every six weeks in winter. In swimming, I do a 400m crawl sub-max, that is, corresponding to a lactate of 4mmol/L (Lactate 4), followed by a 400m at max. In running, I do 3x2000m, the third of which is done at Lactate 4, then a 600m at max. For example I run the first 2000m in seven minutes, the second should be between 20 to 25 seconds faster than the first, and the third 20 to 25 seconds faster than the second, each 2000m being followed by 1min 30sec rest. In cycling, the testing conditions outside are so variable that we have stopped them. Nowadays, I do three to four kilometres on my bike on a turbo trainer. I never do laboratory tests. In fact, three test elements guide me: the stopwatch, lactate and heart rate. So I'm unable to say what my VO_2max is, for example.

Philippe Martin

Why test? In fact, it's a really good idea to analyse strengths and weaknesses. If you don't, you can't devise a coherent training programme. It should be constant (that's implicit), or at least at regular intervals in the course of the season. But what to test? The threshold of each of the disciplines that compose the triathlon. This allows you to refine a grid consisting of six levels, from level one: regeneration, oxygenation (jogging, gentle cycling, swimming technique) to level five (threshold) and six (pure anaerobic, speed)

For running, I use Conconi's treadmill laboratory test. The test starts at a speed of 10kmph, and the speed increases every 200m. Heart rate and lactate are the main points of reference.

Respiratory tests are carried out in a different test where only four levels of speed are used with a 30 sec rest to take blood samples. The steps of this test are worked out so that the last step cannot be finished (giving a total time of 12min). The start of the test can be fixed at 13 to 14kmph, with a 2kmph increase for each step. The speeds are lower for women.

For cycling, I use the Conconi ergocyle test, the triathletes using their own bikes. The test starts with two minutes at 100 Watts, with the power increasing in parallel with the reduction of time, so as to maintain an identical amount of work from step to step. A blood test from the finger is taken with each phase to produce a graph reflecting the lactate levels with each effort.

I don't do any lab test for transitions. In contrast, I have recourse to blood tests to measure lactate (from the finger) and I have observed that in transitions the lactate level often reaches 6 to 8mmol/L, well above the threshold (so Level six).

I also use Conconi as a frame of reference in swimming. The test takes place in the pool and requires good mastery of technique and a careful evaluation of the performance by stopwatch, since it is necessary to improve each 50m by 0.5sec. Heart rate is the indicator in this test (as well as the stopwatch).

In cycling, the road test I use comprises four steps on a flat or uphill course. The length of the shortest effort is three minutes for the last step (so about 4min 30sec for the first). Heart race decides the pace. For example, the rate for the first effort is set at 120, the second at 140, the third at 160 and the fourth at 180. It is the time taken in the intermediate kilometre which allows you not only to compare the in-test performance, but the performance from test to test.

In running, the 5x800m or 5x1000 intervals are carried out on the same principle, using the Fribourg model to determine the threshold.

I test my athletes' strength at Magglingen with Jean Pierre Egger. We target the central muscle groups in order to identify each person's strong and weak points.

Use of heart rate monitors varies depending on the athlete. The heart rate monitor is a very useful aid for the coach, especially when the athlete is inexperienced. Speaking as a coach I would prefer my athletes to wear them in races, but they don't really want to, except over long distances.

Simon Lessing

Testing is needed not only every season, but also after every race. Self evaluation is a constant process. After each race you need to evaluate where you can improve, which parts you need to work on.

Again it is a basic understanding of your body, strengths and weaknesses. So experience of training, travelling and racing with permanent evaluation is the key to performance optimisation.

I have a cardiology test once per year and a blood test every two months, to see if I am lacking any minerals. And that's all. I have done certain tests in the past (VO_2max). I think that once you get a self understanding of your body, you do not need them anymore. That comes down to experience once again.

I don't go out and do a specific field test, to know e.g. how fast I can run a 3000m. The only tests are the races. Training is a different story.

Once again, I know myself. I know I have loads of endurance, and enough speed first. So I'll be concentrating on the first 25 to 50m of the swim.

I always work with a heart rate monitor. But I don't race with it. Heart rate monitors are a useful guide e.g. because fatigue may be physical, motivational or psychological and they help you identify the reason. You can feel fatigued but be able to raise your heart rate to the limits set for your training, meaning you are relatively fresh. Racing is a different story, where you have to constantly adapt to other competitors, and heart rate monitors may conflict with the tactics.

Eduardo No Sanchez

You have to evaluate every day! It is in fact important for you to know if the athlete has slept well, what his heart rate is when he wakes up, how his weight changes, what his feelings are during and after each training session, feelings of tiredness, emotions, pain, etc.

I also try to evaluate my athletes' state of anxiety at regular intervals, their interpersonal relationships, the impact their personal lives have on their sport, how their studies interact with their training, etc. In fact, I spend more time testing my athletes and organising their recovery than training them.

We have recourse to laboratory tests two or three times a year mostly to gauge VO_2max and the aerobic and anaerobic thresholds. On average, our athletes have blood tests every six weeks. On the ground, we do a number of tests aiming to follow changes in lactate levels in swimming, cycling and running. We also use video to analyse technique.

Year after year we repeat the same tests with the same athletes.

In swimming, a distance of 300m serves as my reference point. The athlete's first swim it flat out. Two or three days later they do 5x300m at 89, 91, 93, 95, and 97 percent of their fastest time (1min rest between each repetition). Blood tests are taken after which a graph is drawn which relates times to lactate levels.

In running, I proceed in the same way, the distance of reference being 2000m.

Finally, in cycling, the triathletes in the same way do 5x4km in a velodrome after having established beforehand their record time for the distance.

We use heart rate monitors for all our athletes in triathlon and duathlon, both in training and competition. When drafting was not allowed the heart rate monitor was used for example to choose the most appropriate pedalling frequency. Nowadays, it is an excellent tool for judging the level of concentration of the athletes in the peloton. In fact, perpetual concentration is necessary to make most use of your position in a group, in order to avoid a headwind, to avoid pushing and to have a good race.

Susanne Nielsen

Testing is necessary after every race and at regular intervals during training, to estimate whether the work done has been beneficial or not and whether my coaching has had an effect.

In a laboratory, I do the following test: on an exercise bike I do 5x5min, the speed increasing with each repetition by 3kmph: 25, 28, 31, 34 and finally 37kmph. This first part of the test serves to establish my lactate graph and my actual threshold. When I have reached that threshold I get off the bike and onto the treadmill. I run for five minutes at a moderate pace then increase the speed of the treadmill by 1kmph until I reach my VO_2max. To give an example, I run at 17kmph with a lactate level of 2.5mmol/L.

Outdoors, now and again I have recourse to a time trial to find out how I'm progressing.

I always wear my heart rate monitor! I use it to check the intensity of effort and not to get caught up in sessions which are too hard...or too easy. I might equally have a threshold session of 30min or two hours easy.

Laurent Chopin

It is necessary to test the athletes and it should be systematic.

It forms part of the first part of my training philosophy: it contributes to the athlete's progression (first factor) and it puts the athlete in a competition situation, physically and psychologically (second factor). What is more it allows the coach to learn about the athlete's reactions.

Evaluation tests create the type of stress which has many points in common with a competitive situation. They also let the coach determine the strong and weak points of his athlete. They reflect his line of progression and can result in adjustments in the training phases.

In swimming, I recommend the X times 50m, a test with intervals of 200 and 400m depending on the level of the swimmer, or a series 15 to 20x100m arms only with five to nine seconds recovery. The goal is to clock the best average possible.

In cycling, I do a 6km time trial on a flat course, always the same one, or an intervals test of 3x8min (recovery 3min) with the aim of setting the best average time possible.

In running, I suggest a track test from 1000m to 3000m depending on the level.

The regularity of these tests varies from one sport to another. In running, it is every six weeks. I give precedence to outdoor tests, which to my mind are more essential, over laboratory tests. The coach's feeling, the sensations he experiences in the presence of the athlete, all the subjective impressions which cannot be put into words, help to refine the process of evaluation.

Laboratory tests have a real value, if they are carried out systematically in the same place and following the same procedure. They have a comparative value, comparing test with test, comparing one preparation phase with another and one year to the next.

Some athletes are very keen on these tests, others are more cautious. For my part, I only use them with certain athletes and only to confirm what I observe daily on the ground. Laboratory tests can be interesting in order to evaluate potential or to better understand an athlete you don't know well.

I use the heart rate monitor, but probably much less than in the past. My conversations with certain physiologists and the experience acquired on the ground have made me more reserved in my use of it. I consider it in fact as one more indicator for gauging an athlete's state of being.

According to his heart rate profile from one session to another I can detect, for example, the early stages of overtraining.

The interpretation of graphs certainly gives me invaluable information, but no more than what I get from an athlete's feelings, of the subjective indication of difficulty of a given effort.

From one day to the next, heart rate can fluctuate for reasons independent of training, like, for example, what the athlete has eaten, how he has slept, etc. So it is better not to regard as absolute certainty the information received from a heart rate monitor alone.

To give an example, a track session can be done in the time and frequency demanded, but the athlete might still have found it testing and technically difficult. And if the coach sticks only to the ratio heart rate/time, he might miss a tiredness, a psychological or technical problem. I find that very harmful.

I mainly use the heart rate monitor in the open air. I suggest two types of session to those of my athletes who are preparing for a long distance triathlon.

The first is to develop long distance pace judgement, which is impossible to do on a track and which needs a strong psychological approach: intervals of 3x10min to 3x30min (5min recovery) in a margin of intensity corresponding to 80 to 85 percent of maximum heart rate.

The second aims at avoiding the monotony of a long session by making varying moderate demands. I've called this a bloc session. For example: one hour of running, with ten minutes of running (70 percent of maximum heart rate) plus two minutes at maximum heart rate, all of that repeated five times, but varying the percentages of heart rate according to the coach's or athletes' wishes.

The work phases are made out depending on the evaluation tests and are therefore known to the athletes. But they should be autonomous, and learn how to master and judge their different race paces.

(*) Charles Hadji, *L'évaluation, règles du jeu*, 1989.

CHAPTER SIX

COMPETITION

There is only one morality: to conquer all the obstacles that prevent us from surpassing ourselves.
Louis Pauwels*

Competition in its strictly defined, codified and institutionalised sense is what defines sport, at least in its modern, industrial Coubertin-style version. Without competition, training has no meaning. Without competition there is no career. Without competition there is no battle for supremacy.

Competition is the absolute test, the magical sporting moment, the moment when all these years of practice become flesh.

Competition is a time for records, a settling of scores, the end and the beginning of everything.

A competition is won in a moment, but takes a long time to prepare for. It can take weeks of preparation, but can be played out in the days, hours and minutes which separate the competitor from his moment of truth.

So what happens in a triathlon at the highest level? What is it like from the inside? How is it decided in the hours that precede it? How to sleep, eat and warm-up before a triathlon? How to recover from it, physically and mentally, in the minutes or days that follow? This chapter contains everything you have always wanted to know about competition in the world of the triathlon, from those who live it at the highest level.

Brett Sutton

I don't mind if they don't run the day before a race, but I like them to get on their bike, I like them to feel the pedals, do a couple of 15sec sprints, and they can go 10 km or they can go 40km, it depends on the athletes. Someone like Joanne (King) will ride the bike course the day before (a short triathlon), no matter how hard it is. I like them to feel the pedals because I think they lose the skill very quickly, in the same manner as in swimming. So they would ride and swim, and the run is... they will be walking around anyway, so they are on their legs.

But I am very, very strong in that area: if an athlete says to me: "I want a day off before a race", I say: "don't race". You must understand, you must get a feel for the work, and you must get a feel for the water as for the pedals.

The day before a race would be an active rest. When you swim five kilometres a day, two kilometres is a rest. If you are riding 40 to 80km a day, 20km is a rest. I might give them a day off on Friday, if I think they need it.

Two days before so many people give them sprints, thinking they are sharpening... They are not. They are blunting. You know, doing 25m sprints in a pool two days before a race is simply crazy. Their fast-twitch fibres are going to be dead. They do the same with biking: they get out for short reps of three kilometres or four kilometres just to sharpen up. What it does is that it takes their fast-twitch fibres away. I agree to have our last fast running session 72 hours before a race. I don't disagree with the biking so much. But the swimming is terrible... Any swim coach will tell you that.

The day of the race... You know, there is an enormous difference between Europe and Australia. In Australia, we race at 6:00 in the morning. So when we come over here, our athletes find it very difficult to race at 3:00 in the afternoon. They don't know how to warm up, they don't know how to rest. Usually, when you are starting at 7:00 in the morning, you just get up early, have a little something to eat, go to the race start and try to warm up. What I have done as we've come to Europe is to try to get them out of bed at 7 o'clock. I can't allow them to stay in bed until ten, they would think: "God, isn't France a great place !" It would kill them, they can't race well afterwards. So what I try to do is get them up, and make them have a little jog. So they'll jog for 20 minutes and then have breakfast, and then I try to have them relax again. Then we'll get up again at around 11:00, and have something to eat if the race is at 3:00pm. Then we start to get things organised. You know, even if the next race starts at 9:30am, Emma Carney will get up and go for a run before she races, even if I tell her: "You don't have to, actually". 9 o'clock is late, she would get bored!

Warming up is very difficult from a swim perspective the way the races are. Because if you get them out of the water ten minutes before the start, the warm-up is sort of negligible. They are cold, they even think it hurts them. When some people want to warm up (swimming), I say "OK" because I don't want to upset the mentality, but it is not a warm-up because they get out and they freeze. So if I have people like Joanne, I don't allow her in the water because she'd be hypothermic before she even starts! So we have to pick which people. Ben Bright loves to swim two kilometres before he starts.

I would like them to sit on a wind-trainer if possible to loosen up their legs . I think that's much better than running. I think running in a warm-up, when you get to swim and bike beforehand, has little consequence. I try to get them enough warmth and sweat going for a race start.

The earlier you can do something after a race, the better. Once again, in Australia when we have a race at 6 o'clock, I always call for a training session after 12 o'clock. They'll ride 20 or 30km very easy, I find it is very useful.

Monday (if the race is on Sunday, Author's note) is dedicated to active rest. We won't have a day off straight after the race. We will run, bike and swim on Monday, no matter what. And that's another strong thing the athletes who train with me learn from the coach. If someone is very tired, Tuesday and Wednesday will be used for recovery.

Like Benjamin Bright after Schliersee in 1997 (that year he had competed on three successive weekends, all of the courses were extremely difficult and it was very hot: the

Schliersee and Echternach European cups and the Embrun world cup, Author's note). He worked on Monday after Schliersee, he had Tuesday and Wednesday off, then we built up, we went to Luxembourg (Echternach). His instructions there were to try to do a good job in Embrun the week after Echternach, so if he felt badly during the swim, no matter where his position was, he was not to go hard. In Echternach he swam well, rode well off the pace and dropped out of the run. It was not important because he had put in some good training. But I've brought him to the race (knowing he would not stay with the pace) because this is another thing about being a good coach: had I left him at home, he would have killed himself with training. Because the big problem with Ben is: he just goes until he drops. So I brought him to the race, our sport scientist was there and he was horrified, he said he would be dead for Embrun. I said he would be fantastic (Ben finished third in Embrun world cup that year, Author's note), because he went through the Echternach race aerobically, he ran easy, in control, he did no damage. Had he been at home, he would have been doing hill sprints on the bike, or he would have done a track workout and killed himself. After Embrun, he rode 40km, the next day he rode 40km and swam 5km very slowly, and the next two days nothing.

We had good success in the Formula One grand prix series in Australia (a very short and spectacular circuit with special transitions: double super sprint, eliminator, enduro, etc., Author's note), and we train completely different than anybody else. We train aerobically. I do not take them out and sprint them up, getting them ready for the shorter races. I find that after three races they recover better, they race better, if they train aerobically. If you are a swimmer, when you say to me the race is 20 minutes, it would be 95 percent aerobic, and 5 percent anaerobic. So even little short triathlon races as far as I am concerned can be worked from an aerobic point of view, which makes it safer from an injury point of view. In fact, between each of these F1 races, we do nothing. Just a few sessions at 110bpm to recover because these races are very tiring.

Everyone who prepares specifically for F1 destroys themselves before time and jeopardises their future at the Olympic distance. That's why Brad Beven is no longer any good at it. That's also why I was worried about Magali Messmer (Swiss Magali Messmer finished second in the 1999 and 2000 European championships, Author's note) or Ute Mueckel (one of the fastest swimmers on the circuit, the German Ute Mueckel has divided her career between the short distance and the Ironman, Author's note) who has all the prerequisites to reign over the Olympic distance, but who has strayed into F1. When I think that my training group was just 15 minutes away from Magali's house in Switzerland and that if she had taken the step of contacting me when there was still time, I could have made an Olympic champion of her... (She finished third in Sydney, Author's note) That's why I don't hold to this concept which, moreover, goes around the circuit. I am for the triathlon aerobic sport which tests endurance. These F1 events don't need any cycling ability, they don't interest me.

The problem with the France Iron Tour is not the racing every day, but the travelling, that kills them. I think that the athletes can race four or five times, maybe eight at a go. If the FIT sorts out the transfers all right, I think they can achieve that. It is a great commercial for triathlon. But it has to be put in a situation where it does not wreck the whole season. From my perspective, the people who do the FIT won't do the worlds if the worlds are after the FIT. However, they could do them if the distance of the stages were longer on some days. In recent years, the stages have got shorter and shorter, more and more lactic. If, from time to time, the athletes had the equivalent of a half Ironman they would be able to recover better, since it would really be an aerobic stage.

The other thing is: your heats and finals at the European championships are a wonderful idea. If an athlete has a race on Thursday and cannot back up on Saturday, he is not fit, he should not be here. This is what I was trying to tell Les (Les McDonald, President of the ITU, Author's note): he has got 100 guys going around there when there should not be more than 30 on the start line. If he'd run two heats on Saturday, with the top 15 going through to the final on Sunday, here we are. That's a great commercial for the sport. That is the way to go.

An Olympic triathlon lasts two hours, so it is a very aerobic event. That's the first thing people forget. If you peak for one race, properly, it will take you two months to do the next race. Our sport is so young that most coaches and athletes don't understand it. This is a real problem, but how would you know? We have no tradition in triathlon because the top guys are still here after eight years. Dave Scott came back at 45. Why do these guys still beat the young ones? So I look at myself as a coach and say: "You are a failure at the present moment". We are on a great learning curve for our sport. We don't have the 50 years of history running's had, nor the 100 years swimming has had. So we are still learning what's the best way.

Grégoire Millet

In the days before a competition we do the least work possible. If competition day falls on a Sunday, we don't do anything serious on Saturday (familiarise ourselves with the circuits, or do short running intervals). On Friday we don't do anything. Thursday is given over to phase three work (maximum aerobic speed work) like the following: swimming 3x3x100m, every two minutes; running 6x200m or 4x300m. One hour cycling (spinning) may also be done to act as a warm-up.

Before the race... that depends on the timetable. If the race is in the morning, first you have to get up in good time... then have a good ride (I don't favour running warm ups) for example: cycle for 20 minutes followed by an out-of-the-water swim warm-up, the sort you would do by the side of the pool is enough. I don't particularly agree with swimming before a triathlon. The start of the race is lactic and you have to prepare for that, but you also have to bear in mind that the glycogen will be seriously brought into play so you should not overdraw it too soon. I don't like long warm-ups unless the race is late in the day. In this case I favour a good training session in the morning corresponding to half a typical training session. For example, a short swimming session (if the training conditions lend themselves to it) and 30 to 35km on the bike.

Post-race recovery

On the same day, a cool-down session is necessary, but that often does not happen for many reasons. I impose it on the athletes only when there is another race immediately afterwards, three days later for example. A lot of triathletes do it systematically, by riding for an hour, for example. In the days following, from Tuesday, I programme intermittent running, because slow intermittent work does not deplete glycogen so much as continuous work. I also choose it for technical, stylistic reasons.

To resume running training after a triathlon, I apply a simple principle: one day (globally) of recovery for each 10km. In other words, after the Olympic distance an athlete can run again on Tuesday, after a middle distance on Wednesday, after Nice the athlete can go do a little jogging Thursday and after Hawaii I wait for the end of the week before suggesting any running.

In principle, I am against having a succession of races (whether it be the world cup every week, the system of qualifying rounds and final in the European championships, or the France Iron Tour) which overload the system to a great extent. I understand the political, broadcasting and financial reasons behind putting the races close together but none of these reasons is in favour of the athlete's physical health.

You start to build a peak ten weeks before the aim in question. I hope to reach it essentially using altitude. And I rely on the models and existing data in order to plan this peak: the delay in the decline in aptitude which lasts about 40 to 50 days, the delay in the decline in energy levels which lasts about ten to 15 days, and the length of time after going back down to sea level which is around 17 to 20 days. You also have to bear in mind that athletes react differently to altitude and that you should as a consequence programme the return to sea level differently for each competitor.

Isabelle and Béatrice Mouthon

(Béatrice and Isabelle) The night before a race (whether short distance or long) it's a habit (but not an obligation) to practise the three disciplines: relaxed swimming, ride with occasional bursts of speed, increasing cadence to get the pulse up and easy running with a few accelerations (6) of 15-20 seconds duration. The total sum of these sessions does not exceed two hours to two hours 30 minutes. This is why we always arrange it so that we arrive at the competition site two days before the race, which corresponds to our rest day. We travel the night before only if it is a short distance. Training the day before a race gives us a chance to have a look at the course, which is not always possible (in swimming for example) for technical reasons. Our priority is always the cycling course, although sometimes the run also needs special attention. So sometimes we cover the course on a bike.

If we are in place for a week, it is possible for us to have a light session two days before the race. This is not for training purposes, but just to give us something to do. In this case, it's just a jog before breakfast for 30 minutes, or relaxed swimming, or a short spin on the bike.

In any case, we are in favour of doing a lot of stretching and especially two days before the race, since we have a lot of time on our hands.

If it's a long distance race, the pre-race warm-up is not really an issue. Apart from a bit of swimming in order not to be surprised.

Before an Olympic distance race, we go out for a spin for about 15 kilometres with a few accelerations, or we do two to three kilometres jogging if our bikes are already checked-in at the transition area. But the priority is always a warm-up on the bike.

Finally, we never train on race day, even if the race is late in the day.

The ideal active recovery after a race is ten to 15km on the bike, very easy, low gears, and taking on a lot of water. Otherwise, we do a lot of stretching again and have massage if it's available (and professional) and we use our Compex in the evening.

The two days that follow are 'cool', and even more so Tuesday than Monday. On Monday we swim (3 to 4km easy, working on technique) and we ride (spin, easy) but we do not run. Tuesday we run easy for 30, 40, or 50 minutes and we swim, but we do not ride. On Wednesday we resume the difficult sessions.

(Béatrice) At certain times in the season I do four races in three weeks. So I don't have much time for quality sessions and, naturally, my priority is recovery. Physical, mental and nervous recovery so that I can confront the next race. In fact, in this context there are only two days in the week when any specific quality work can be carried out: Wednesday and Thursday. The sessions are shorter and in the form of intervals. For example, instead of doing a pure track session (400m) I do diagonals on the football pitch which are less demanding. It is only in swimming that you can allow yourself intense intervals from Tuesday onwards (and even up to Friday) which means you don't have to do them Wednesday and Thursday which is allotted first and foremost to the harder cycling and running sessions between two race weekends.

(Isabelle and Béatrice)

A peak in form exists but you never know when it is in time, even if you train specifically to reach it on D-day. A peak is a bit of an abstract concept, whereby you surpass yourself physically and mentally.

To reach it, we spend three weeks at altitude and have a race the weekend or two weeks before the main objective. Not a particularly big race, and over the Olympic distance if we are getting ready for a middle distance triathlon, and a sprint if we are preparing for an Olympic distance race. You have to do races which are not mentally draining in the weeks which precede the main objective.

Nutrition is equally important for us, especially if we are peaking for a long distance race. We keep to the Dissociated Scandinavian Regime which is a way of motivating ourselves to be at the top of our physiological capacity on D-day (see chapter: Nutrition and diet).

Karen Smyers

If I race on Sunday (short distance) I continue doing intensity until Tuesday or Wednesday: 6x400m or (800m + 2x400m) running, aimed at sharpening but not getting tired. 6 or 7x2min peak-ups on the bike.

Both sessions may be done the same day or on two consecutive days. I have discovered that the biking can be done a little bit closer to the race. For the swim, I am cutting back on total distance (3.5km) from Wednesday. The last run would be on Thursday. I swim 2000m on Friday, together with an easy spin on the bike. On Saturday, a little swim to stay loose and a 30min bike ride. If the race is on Sunday morning, I will not wake up earlier than two hours before the start.

Everything is packed and ready the day before. I would get into the transition area one hour before the start, and I do a ten to 15min bike ride, I run about 10min and I warm up by swimming just before the start. For an afternoon start (let's say 1pm), I get up at 8am usually and have a very light breakfast with coffee. I drink a lot of water maybe also an electrolyte drink. I don't do any warming up until one hour before the race.

Generally, I don't do anything until the end of the day. For the Ironman, forget about cooling down. The press conference is the only thing I can do well! A two hour effort in triathlon is not a 5-mile run, where I build a lot of lactic acid. It is just different.

I do an easy bike ride and swim the next day. I can go right into intensity in running again as early as Tuesday. I swim hard on Wednesday and do bike intervals on Thursday.

Sometimes I do have to reorganise my training to accommodate days off, due to travel or sponsors' obligations. I do not plan them, I just figure out they are going to happen and are probably good for me in the long run.

I try to race a maximum of two races a month (1991 was an exception, with 21 races, when I won the world cup). If I race three times in a month, I cut down on what I am doing in between races because the races become a big part of my weekly intensity.

You can't do too many races for too many months in a row, you don't have a big enough block of time where you can really keep up your base.

I compete in 12 to 15 races, between April and November, with two long distance races: Hawaii and Nice or Zofingen for example.

Reaching a peak is not really different in triathlon than in any other sport. You are just tapering in three sports instead of one. You build enough endurance, then you gradually introduce some speed where your body gets faster and faster and as you decrease the distance you get tuned to the speed, then comes the moment where you'll be at your fastest point. You have to decrease the mileage enough to let your body be really fast but without reaching the point where you have decreased your mileage so much that you are getting out of shape.

Lothar Leder

Before short races, I always do some speed work in the week to get sharp, and some transition work the day before: a 20km hard bike ride and then a 10min run (5 min flat out and 5min easy, making 3km).

The structure of training in the week preceding a short race depends on where you are, what the training facilities are, what the team does, etc. In fact, it is not really fixed for me.

For long races, however, it is fixed. The weekend before, I have a last long (30km) run. If I am really fit, I do it fast (meaning 4min/km pace), if not I do it easier. From this moment on I don't run further than 10km. If the race is on Sunday, I do a long bike ride (150km) on Tuesday but not too fast. My last training before an Ironman takes place the day before when I do all three sports for 20 minutes: 20min cycling, 20min swimming, 20min running. I have a rest day two days before competition. The rest of the week I train how I feel. If I feel like doing nothing, I do nothing. Too many people get too stressed the final week. For me it's the opposite. I take pleasure in eliminating all forms of stress.

The last week before an Ironman, I sleep in in the morning: in Roth, you have to get up really early in the morning, something like 3 o'clock, so I train for it in the last week. I get up at 3am, watch TV for two to three hours, I have breakfast and go back to sleep. Same with Hawaii where I have to wake up at 4 o'clock. If you don't train for it, you get very nervous when the bell rings. It is a new situation, your body cannot deal with it. So I do it for three to four days, unless I am really tired.

If the race is in the afternoon, I do a 30min wake up run, have breakfast and go back to sleep. Then I do my warm up starting one-and-a-half hours before the race. If the race is in the morning, I only warm up one hour before the race. Warm up is not too hard: bike 20min, run 10min up and down, and some push-ups before the swim. I do not carry a windtrainer with me, so if the bike has to be racked in the transition area long before, I simply do not bike, I only run. Regarding the swim warm-up, since I am not a good swimmer I have been watching what others were doing... If you watch Simon Lessing, he sits there in his wetsuit, doing nothing for the last 20 min but putting his feet in the water, not even stretching, so you get really confused! Brad Beven, on the other hand, is doing his stretch cord like crazy. I tried it and it does not work for me. So I'll keep trying everything until I find the right warm-up for me.

After a short course race, I go for a bike ride or a run. I prefer a run, it is better. You don't want to run after a race, but you should go for an easy 30min jog. Half-an-hour is a good amount, to be able to get rid of the lactate, and to train more and better the next day and week.

You run hard at the end of a triathlon, so you need to recover actively. If you can get your bike and you have nice people around, you can go for a 30 minute bike ride cool-down. This is what I do sometimes in France with my club.

If I have a journey the day after a race, I do not train. I always try to travel the day after the race. Then I feel really good on Tuesday and start with a long bike ride to have a base for the week. To get back into the swimming is the hardest part for me. After a race I do not swim good. That means that I have to swim everyday.

I saw Natascha Badmann run in the morning the day after Hawaii... I could never do that. I am glad to get to my car, pick up my bike at the transition area and leave. The next day, anyway, I cannot walk. I am really dead. I have experienced a bike ride (one-and-a-half-hour mountain bike) the next day after my victory and world record in Roth. I felt really positive and could train then. This is why Brett Sutton does it: if you win, you are really on a high and you can train, even hard, it does not bother you. It works. But I prefer to do nothing for one week after the Ironman. Nothing at all. After the Ironman, your body is so tired that even if you swim... your body starts freezing. I do nothing. You simply eat a lot because your body is like a sponge.

In 1997 I did Roth and went straight to the world cup race in Stockholm afterwards where I recorded the third fastest run split. How I did it was... no training at all during the days between Roth and Stockholm, meaning therefore no run. I ran only for 30min the day before the race. And drafting was allowed so it was not that hard to get to the run. In fact, I did the same between Hawaii and Sydney: I flew from Kona, where I had a great race, to Europe and from Europe to Australia, and then again recorded a top-3 run split. I do crazy things to find out about myself. And sometimes it does not work. For example, in 1998 after Hawaii I went for a run race at the Nurburgring, and I ran like a snail. I got beaten by fat people!

First of all, you can only do a lot of triathlons in a row if you have accumulated a lot of base work in the springtime. It is always the same rhythm from week to week: the beginning of the week is recovery, mid-week is dedicated to fast stuff (intervals in running, maybe on the bike too), and then the routine of the last three days, including the day off at D-day minus two, and the little warm-up at D-day minus one. With this approach, I can only hope to be good in three consecutive races, because then I am tired. And I'd be at my best for the second and third races.

I have done the France Iron Tour several times, but it is difficult to say anything about it, because I have always done it when I was tired.

At the beginning, peaking is a mental task, you have your goal in your mind. Then you prepare the other things around it: training, private life, food, travelling, etc. It needs a number of years before being able to peak properly for a goal, to be able to overcome the overall pressure surrounding it.

Luc Van Lierde

The biggest difference between the week preceding a long triathlon and a short one is the recovery. You can continue training for a short race while for the long race the order of the day is recovery! Before Hawaii, I train for a maximum of two hours a day and it is not a problem if I do nothing for the two days before the race. The day before I just do a little swimming.

On the other hand, you can go for a bike ride lasting two or three hours the day before or two days before a short race. And that is also true in swimming as well as cycling and running. It's a question of muscle tone, which is more necessary for the short distance triathlon. So I train every day of the week of a short distance race. The day before a short triathlon, I train for two to three hours, often in the three sports. In fact, I train for the three sports five days a week, as opposed to three for the long distance.

For a short triathlon, I train one-and-a-half hours before the start: I ride for 30 minutes, run for ten to 15 minutes, and swim for about ten minutes just before the race. Whether the triathlon is in the morning or the afternoon. For long distance, however, swimming is the warm-up. The conditions are, in fact, completely different between a short triathlon, which lasts no longer than two hours of sometimes extremely lactic effort, and Hawaii where the 3.8km swim is nothing more than the beginning of a very long day.

After the European championships short distance, I swam, rode and ran for recovery after the semi-finals because the final was not until two days later. In contrast, after the final I did nothing at all. When I have a race the following week, I always try to run after the event for 15 to 20 minutes. It would of course be better to go for a ride but the bikes are still embargoed in the transition area. I start serious training again two days after a short triathlon.

At the end of an Ironman I don't see how anyone can run! I give the first three recovery days over to swimming. From the fourth day on I cycle and I don't run until after a week.

I have done three ITU races as well as the European championships in the space of five weeks. The mileage was completed in its entirety before the first race in the series. The first two days after each race were given over to recovery and the rest of each week was punctuated by short intense sessions. Depending on how the previous race went, the intensive sessions are given over to one activity or another. For example, if my swimming technique was not good the weekend before I will do speed sessions in swimming the following Thursday and Friday. If on the other hand I swam well, but my running lacked rhythm, I'll do an intensive running session.

There are people who hit their peak, and there are others who never manage it. I started sport with swimming which is all about peaks, because there are not many big races each year. You have to start very early thinking about peaking so that you can get used to it and so that it happens.

Philippe Martin

Up to two days before (or the day before) a race, swimming training functions at 80 percent of volume in zones two and three. The last decent session is done three days before the race and a few minutes are given over to it the day before. In cycling, the route is looked at two or three days before the race. Finally, a very modest session is carried out the day before (a few minutes of running).

The last really intense session for each of the three disciplines takes place one week before the race. This can be a problem when the races are every week.

Warm up varies depending on the competitor. I recall an athlete who was so nervous before a race that I told him to go for a 20km ride to calm himself down and relax. On the other hand, listening to music is ideal. This is where ritual is useful.

You have to swim to warm up for a triathlon, which is something athletes don't necessarily appreciate. They often prefer to go for a run. Everything in fact depends on the climate. In Cancun, two minutes is enough, in Zundert, a lot more…

After a race, I advocate one to two hours on the bike in zone one on the day of the race and the following day, nothing. Is recovery different after a short race compared to a long one? I don't think so. Look at Natascha Badmann, she goes for a ride after Hawaii as well as Zofingen.

I do not advocate doing successive races. If an athlete has to do three races in three weeks he should be very well prepared. The training load should be reduced each week to help recovery. However, it is not a good idea to make this a firm rule, because many variations can be seen depending on the athlete. As for qualifying rounds and final which is what you get in the European Triathlon and Duathlon championships, you have to train the whole week. The athlete sticks to his individual training plan the whole week preceding the championships. He has a day of rest (to find his way around the courses) three to five days before the event. The day after the semi-final, our duathletes do almost nothing (for example, ten to 15 minutes running), but the triathletes do swimming at least.

Simon Lessing

The days preceding a race, I usually cut back on training. I am the sort of athlete who does not like to take time off. If you stop too long before a race, you lose the touch, the sensation that you have been striving for the race. My option is to cut down from three sports to two sports a day, take it easy with short 30min runs, or a short 2km swim. There is less intensity short sprint stuff.

I definitely prefer to race in the afternoon or the evening. The worst part of racing in the morning is that you get a bad night of sleep and there is no time to warm up, to take your time, to concentrate on what you are doing. You are literally getting out of your bed and jumping into the water, which is a real shock for the body.

For a warm up, I definitely do stretching beforehand. I do not really like to run. Occasionally I'll go for a short bike ride when I have the opportunity. I definitely like to swim for at least 800m, when the water is warm enough. I want to check that I am not diving into anything that is going to be a surprise. I do not like the element of surprise. I want to know what to expect when the gun goes off. I think the swim start is the most critical part of a triathlon, with this mass of people dashing on each other.

To be honest, I don't do much after a race. I like to get back to my hotel and have a shower. But it depends on how your racing has been. If your legs feel really tired, you have to go for a warm down. I like electro-stimulation machines which I find really great for warming down. This is good because you are not getting your heart rate up, but are still moving your muscles.

Usually I take a day off after the race. I like to be just doing an easy swim, or easy run or easy bike, but not too much. Take it easy really and get back to serious things on Tuesday. I still feel a little flat two days after a race, but I really feel better on the third day. So if the race is on Sunday, I'll take it easy on Monday. I'll do all three disciplines on Tuesday but nothing intense, and Wednesday I'll have pretty much recovered from the race.

My rule before used to be: one day off completely. But obviously now we have to deal with travelling, and a lot of time when you have no possibility to train. For me I would regard that as a day off. In fact it all depends on how much time you have, on what races you are doing and where you are doing them.

I don't like to actually race four weeks in a row but I think two weeks in a row is great. I definitely have more sensation on the second weekend. I'll go for a sprint or an Olympic distance race the weekend before a main objective, depending on how my training is, how many races I have done beforehand.

Once again it comes down to consistency. If you are racing every two weeks consistently throughout the season, it is fine. But when you go through a long period of time without racing (for example in 1997, where I had no race between the London Triathlon on September 16 and the worlds in Perth in November), I specifically look to do intermediate races.

Eduardo No Sanchez

I don't train the whole national squad the whole year. On the other hand, I follow all the squad members in the days prior to competition. Usually, for an important race, we do a long transition with seven days to go: 80 to 90km ride, with the last 30km easy, followed by a more-or-less long run, always beginning with 15 minutes hard (based on 9min 10sec for 3000m for the men) followed by ten to 15 minutes at a moderate pace. We don't do anything day five and 48 hours before the race. Day four we do volume and day three rhythm sessions (not too intense) with long recovery.

If the race takes place in the afternoon, we do the equivalent of a triathlon in the morning: often a 1500m swim to start with, then 30 to 40 minute ride. Some athletes like to run in the morning before breakfast, but not everybody. After this session, the athletes have a shower, get their gear ready and go to the competition site. They do a normal warm-up, including a ride until the first sweat breaks out. Then they get off their bikes and run at pace with one or two bursts. Finally, they swim 1000m, changing pace if possible and finish off with some stretching. So, in total, the athletes train two to two hours 15 minutes before an afternoon competition.

If the race is in the morning, the last training session takes place the day before and lasts one to two hours. In the 30 minutes following the effort, my athletes drink diluted apple juice in varying amounts between one and two litres, depending on competitors and the races. And in the hour that follows the race, they get together and go off for an hour's ride to recover.

The day after a race, the athletes have a gentle training session in all three disciplines. They also spend a lot of time (45 minutes to one hour) stretching. The next day, the juniors do absolutely nothing while the elite train easy. The third day, one of the three disciplines is practised (most often swimming or cycling) with a certain intensity, but not the other two. When there are several triathlons in a row, the inter-competitive sessions are short and intense (speed) and the recovery periods very long.

In the specific case of the European championships (where the qualifying rounds for the sprints are on Thursday and the final on Saturday over the Olympic distance, Author's note) the three disciplines are practised on Friday, two of them on Saturday, warming up (two hours) and recovery (30km cycling, 1000 to 1500m swimming, stretching 45 minutes, massage and osteopathy with the use of essential oils).

Susanne Nielsen

The week before a short triathlon, I at least halve my threshold work, even more for running than cycling. However, I always run threshold for at least 15 minutes, so as to conserve the feeling for this pace in competition. In terms of volume, the reduction in work is equivalent to about 40 percent. I try to sleep as long as possible the night before the race (that of course, depends on when it starts). I shave, have a shower and eat a little three hours before the race: a banana and two pieces of bread, and drink a carbohydrate mix until one hour before the race. In the hour before, I'll drink only water.

My warm up (very limited) includes stretching (often in the hotel), sometimes a little running, but I prefer, if possible, to cycle for five or six kilometres. After a triathlon, I always drink a lot. If I feel good, I immediately try to go out for a ride for an hour at the most. If I'm really tired I have a shower and try to sleep a little.

I'm capable of doing three races in three weekends in a row, then I have to rest for a weekend before starting the next series of three races. Nowadays, however, I run less than in the past, because I'm more motivated by a limited number of aims.

You can, of course, work on peaks, that's what I do all through the year. If I train a lot for two or three weeks and then train less, I will reach a peak. When I'm preparing for a major goal, I test my form two to three weeks before the date.

Laurent Chopin

What is planned before a race depends on the athlete concerned and the relative importance of the competition.

Before an important objective the structure of training is always the same:

Monday: aerobic session swimming, running.

Tuesday: aerobic session swimming, race pace cycling plus running 10x100m strides.

Wednesday: short running session at maximum aerobic speed.

Thursday: recovery on the bike, short swimming session, technical work and 12x25metres at 30sec intervals (two lengths quick, one length easy).

Friday: complete rest.

Saturday: 45min cycling along the course, 4x1min, 1min at maximum aerobic strength, 25min running on the course, 6x15sec/15sec.

Sunday: triathlon

Before a non-goal oriented competition, training depends on the athlete and the point he has reached in his preparation. In any case, the triathlon represents the 'race pace' of the week.

The day of competition starts with 30min muscular activity of the athlete's choice depending on his form and the discipline he chooses. The pre-race warm-up consists of the reconnaissance of the entry and exit from the transition area, either on foot or by bike, and of the traffic flow through the area. I always recommend swimming when it is possible (according to the water temperature). If not, we will have a dry swim warm up (using a stretch cord if the athlete has one).

If the water temperature is fine, swimming for at the most a quarter-of-an-hour after the race is ideal. Since that is unfortunately rarely possible in France, I ask my athletes to go for a spin for 15 to 20 minutes. I avoid jogging for fear of injury.

The next day and the day after that very often follow the same pattern:

Monday: recovery swimming, bike 1hr 15min to 1hr 30min recovery.

Tuesday: swimming (short session), easy jogging.

If the race was a key objective, the four days following a race are free. There should be no constraints on the athlete. He should be allowed to blow out if he wants and at his own pace.

If the goal was not reached, I meet the athlete or contact him by phone to analyse the reasons for the failure. That said, I have noticed that the athletes that normally train with me often do in these four days what I would have asked them to do. And since they decide the content of that, they give it even more importance.

I place special importance on nutrition and hydration with my athletes during the recovery period. I also recommend a visit to the physio, a good sauna or a Jacuzzi.

After a long distance triathlon, I let a complete week of recovery go by, giving the same instructions to the runners. The resumption of training will take place very progressively and no big physiological demands are made in the two following weeks.

So it seems a little unreasonable to compete in a long and short triathlon within three weeks especially if you are looking for good results. Lothar Leder has shown us that it is within the bounds of possibility by finishing on the podium in Roth and some days later in the top ten in a world cup event. You can equally ask yourself what he would have done had he not competed in Roth…

Lothar is certainly the exception that proves the rule. For my part, with the best physical and mental interests of my athletes at heart, I try to avoid demands of this type.

It is difficult to control this aspect in the training programme. When the events are too close together you risk exposing yourself to the phenomenon of losing form or, if the recovery is not enough, to over-training. So you have to be vigilant on this point.

When the races are close together, my classic plan is the following: Monday, Tuesday: as usual. Wednesday, Thursday: physiological maintenance. Friday, Saturday: as usual.

In this situation, competition constitutes the race pace sessions. Over a short period, this could be said to suffice to maintain form.

I cannot conceive of four races in a row because my method of training is based on the fact that it is impossible to be 100 percent for four weekends in a row. In consequence, if you are going to do this, you have to treat each race differently. It's all about success for the athlete. In that sense, I would focus on one particular race compared to which the others would be reference points with mental coaching before and after the target event.

Peaking corresponds to the physiological and psychological optimisation of the athlete. This peak is a little abstract and difficult to reach in a triathlon which, above all, is the aggregate of three disciplines. And since, finally, a peak has two faces, one ascending, the other descending.

For my part, I don't use charts, save those which follow on from running tests carried out on the track.

(*) Louis Pauwels, *Blumroch l'admirable ou le déjeuner du surhomme*, 1978.

CHAPTER SEVEN

TRANSITIONS

Transitions are a great race simulation, you get really aggressive and quicker in the transitions. And if something goes wrong in a race you can deal with it. You feel really self-confident if you accumulate a lot of transitions training before a race! Lothar Leder.

In the course of the years that followed the invention of modern triathlon in California (when the USA 'discovered' the triathlon, at Fiesta Island 1975, then imposed it on the rest of the whole world thanks to Hawaii, organised in 1978, France already had a 50-year history in this discipline, through numerous diverse activities known under the evocative names: The Three Sports, The Smart Race, The Try-Everything Sport, Author's note), triathlon training consists of training in each of the three sports.

At the end of the eighties, a new mode of training emerged and was developed. It included specific sessions which served as cement for the training programme in this discipline: transitions.

'Bricks' and 'super bricks', 'Koppeltraining', 'multi-enchaînements'… so many variations on the same concept which multiplied throughout the world and produced an infinite variety of activity, according to what the transitions are, the duration and intensity of effort, the number of transitions, the time of year when these transitions are programmed, etc.

Certain coaches and athletes swear by transitions. Others claim they have never done them. Finally, others make use of them in moderation, at certain special times of their season.

Who is telling the truth? All of them, no doubt, after their fashion. Form your own opinion!

Brett Sutton

I do them the whole year, except going into a race. They are more stressful so I would drop off the bricks ten days out from the world championships. Hopefully we would 'have it in the bank'. We are not trying to do any catch-up work in the last week. If you get to ten days before the worlds and it is not all put away, cleaned up and ready to go, you haven't done a good job and you're wasting your time.

That said, if a particular athlete feels good running off the bike, me being the top coach I am (smiles), I reply: "Yes, of course, it's great training. Let's do it". If they say to me: "Chief, on Wednesday I just know I need to run 4km easy off the bike, I would say: "That's exactly what I had in mind". I might not have had that in mind, but what I had in mind, going into the world championships... Never upset the mentality, especially in those moments.

In my own opinion, bricks take a little more energy, so I would not give a brick too close to a race.

The other part of the brick philosophy is that I have no problem with them doing a longer set. So where the French make their long ride of four to five hours, we might do a brick of four hours. They might swim for an hour-and-a-half, and then go riding for two hours rather than four. That's why we are able to fit the brick in. We might run for an hour and then swim for an hour-and-a-half. Even though this is not a traditional triathlon brick, this is what true triathlon is. People have to realize that to swim after you ran is a difficult thing, and if you are not a swimmer you can't do it, or if you're not a trained person it is difficult. In Australia, we do a couple of those races where they swim-bike-run, swim-bike-run, so it is important to be able to run and then to swim. So we would incorporate that and call that a brick.

We do a swim-bike brick once a week, we would do a bike-run brick, and we would do a run-swim brick. We don't do multi-bricks. I have done that. I can assure you: it kills them, it overtrains them. We used to do seven kilometres on the bike and then jump off and do 1km run, and do five of them. Very exciting, very fast, good on the stop-watch, but for four days after everything else was shit. So I thought: "Well, we can get away with that". But you can't get away with that, because then you lose the tempo of your training programme. So I cut it back to three and found that the athletes were running faster after the bike. Straight away, I was really excited because like all coaches I like to see good times at training. And then I found that the times in racing were not as good as the times in training. And there were some occasions where they were saying: "Coach, I feel tired, even if we are not doing any work." And that scared me. And I stopped that kind of session.

Another one that people do a lot of is 2x(20km bike and 5km run). It just seems to drain them, and I don't want to drain them, I want them to be tired but also to be able to come back the next day and do something that is beneficial.

So we would ride on the bike and jump off and do a 4km. If they were feeling badly they would run very slowly, if they feel ok, they could go whatever speed they would like. We would sometimes only ride very short (half-an-hour), and then run 12 to15 km. And once again we would do it whichever way they feel good. Some would smash the bike and do the run as a recovery, others would go easy on the bike, and jump off for a solid 12km. It's got to be your athlete's decision, because we can't get inside their body and see how they feel.

I know Ben (Bright) does a set where he runs 6km, then he rides for 45 minutes, then he does a 6km run. He does it how he feels, and it makes him feel so good to do that session. No stop-watch.

I think you have got to train as you race. If I had a race that has multiple transitions all the time, we would change the training. As I said, in Australia we have maybe more practical reference because we have a race series that has got a lot of money, so the athletes have to do well. And I found that athletes who do multiple training and changes don't do as well as the athletes who are training on a longer aerobic system. A guy like Benjamin Sanson (former elite swimmer, he started triathlon at the beginning of the nineties and has had a successful career without winning anything big up to the present time, Author's note) should win these races, but he does not, certainly because of the way he approaches them. And I guess it is for the same reason that Olivier Marceau (European Junior champion in 1992, Olivier Marceau became world champion in Australia 2000, Author's note) did not succeed when he came over for the winter some years ago.

Grégoire Millet

It's a very interesting approach for future athletes: seniors who are beginning the triathlon or juniors. It seems to me pedagogically worthwhile to organise transitions in a stadium with home-trainers. That said, if you are looking to create the race conditions specific to a triathlon it is better to avoid home-trainers which do not recreate the sensory conditions of a race. I hold to the concept, in its fundamentally playful meaning (the bike-run is a very good example of it).

I like to suggest transitions which alternate physiological work in cycling with technical work in running. For example: six minutes of threshold training with a home-trainer, 100m bounding, 200m at a good speed, and 300m fast. Or during very specific sessions (like hill sessions): interval hill training on the bike, or false flat running (super speed work). In Montpellier we have a two-kilometre hill and a false flat downhill that we mark out every 50 metres. In these sessions the athletes climb the hill together at a good speed, park their bikes and continue with technical work running on a false flat downhill: first 50 metres unwinding, then shortening each 50m by three strides.

I do simple transitions but not the multi-transition, even though the structure of my sessions approaches them sometimes. For example, I can do a home-trainer-running technique transition several times, but the athletes will always rest before starting on the next session. I also do swimming-running transitions on the beach, in May, for example. All these transitions get you into shape very quickly to the extent that they are carried out at high speed.

As such, I make the athletes do transitions in the pre-competition period. But I can just as easily make them do them in winter for technical reasons. In the case of the home-trainer-running transition, I create the conditions of pre-fatigue with movements which are not suited to running, in order to reinforce the difficulty of maintaining running technique: opening up the hip, working the gluteus. Here I apply the contrasting method by associating cycling practice to a series of muscular exercises, for example.

Personally, I do not believe in transitions as base work. What is more, I am not sure of the point of it, to the extent where the work carried out to this day on the subject has not involved the elite. So no beneficial conclusion can be reached for the elite. Finally, transitions potentially make athletes run the risk of over-training or of suffering extra injury, something which the athletes definitely do not need.

That said, I do transitions, because it is an excellent way of approaching the special characteristics of the discipline.

Isabelle and Béatrice Mouthon

(Béatrice and Isabelle) Transitions help you above all to get your body used to changing position, and using other muscle groups. When you get off your bike after your first triathlon, you are really disturbed. With training we now have the impression that we are capable of running faster getting off the bike than when we only did running. So it is vital to do transitions.

In France, it is very difficult to do specific swimming-cycling transitions, because we don't have the infrastructure and because legislation concerning swimming pools does not allow you to have bikes by the side of the pool. In Australia, we were able to train at this swimming-cycling transition, which is excellent, because the arms are mainly used in swimming and immediately afterwards the blood has to flow to the legs again to gain maximum power without delay.

In fact, in Australia we have done all sorts of transitions, swimming-running and cycling-swimming, which has been very interesting for us in the sense of maximum adaptability. In general, we have very much enjoyed the competitive nature of these sessions.

Another interesting point lies in the better management of equipment and technique in transitions: getting on and off the bike, putting on your shoes, etc. So many details which acquire enormous importance in the world cup and in all the events where drafting is allowed.

Transitions are very beneficial, but also very demanding, more in any case than the separate practice of the disciplines. You should not, then, make too much use of them. In the past we did a lot of transitions (one a week). Nowadays, the tests we have done with Grégoire have shown us that we have completely assimilated these transitions. Our second run was even more economic than the first and our stride did not collapse at all. Also, we no longer really see the need to do transitions. At the very most, at the start of the season, we do some sessions to remind ourselves, above all with the home-trainer and track combination.

When a track session is programmed, we begin almost systematically with an hour of home-trainer with some (6 to 10) short sprints (20sec) and super fast cadence (120 rpm), and then we do track with very little warm up. The track session can be very varied but never exceeds 5000m.

(Isabelle) I recently did a very interesting transition including a mixture of pace one (base work) with diagonals which went off very well.

I think there's a connection between pedal cadence and stride frequencies. When we started with high spin bike sessions it became easier to have higher stride frequency.

We noticed the same phenomenon when we were using a fixed gear. This speed is ideal at the beginning of a run, even if we lose it a little in the course of a session.

It is, besides, interesting to note that more and more runners get on the bike and find that it is good training psychologically, because they can reduce their running mileage.

Transitions can injure you and lead to over-training. So you have to modulate the sessions, and consider, for example, the bike sequences as recovery, or the runs, or a part of each, thereby having active recovery sequences in the midst of transition sessions.

Karen Smyers

In short races, I practice bike-to-run transitions at the beginning of each season. However, I have done triathlon for so many years now that my body responds really quickly to that kind of training.

The swim-to-bike transition is not a problem because the muscle groups involved are not that incompatible with switching.

Transition is a learned response to get your quads loose enough to get into a running motion right away. So I do a couple of work-outs before my first race. Not too many (if any) because I find it tiring. I might do a bike ride and then an easy run. Hard bike-to-run sessions are saved for races except prior to the season's start.

When I train for long distance, I often do a long bike ride on Saturday, followed by an easy 20 to 30min run.

Lothar Leder

Transitions are a great race simulation, you get really aggressive and quicker in the transitions. And if something goes wrong in a race you can deal with it. You feel really self-confident if you accumulate a lot of transitions training before a race. To put your glasses, helmet, and shoes on becomes normal and does not bother you anymore, you can concentrate more on your swim, bike and run. In Australia, I learned from Col and Miles Stewart that to train the transitions better you need to get a bad spot in the transition area where your bike is, then if you have a good bike spot in the race you are like Terminator, you are really fast.

Another thing that I learned is that you need a lot of rest after a session of transitions. In Australia, I tell you: on Thursday transitions, on Friday, day off. And after the transitions on Thursday in the afternoon, nothing. You go and see movies.

I prefer the Enduro type, where you swim 200m, bike 5km and run 1km, which you do three times without recovery, and you try to be faster each time. If the group is good, you go flat out the last one. It is really like a race.

You go easily too fast (a lot of people, especially the juniors, push too hard), and because of this you lose your technique. When I was in Australia, if Miles Stewart was in the group, it was not fun. With him, you have to do the transitions like you never race, he is not fooling around, he is really fast, and if you sleep then you do not catch the train and you cycle on your own.

Another limit is that it is too cold in Germany to think of doing transitions in the winter time, and too much of an arsehole anyway here. I do only bike-to-run transition, and not often. Swim to bike is too difficult: you have to run out of the pool, you have to ask the pool staff to open the door, and people look at you strangely if you run out of the park half naked... it is too much.

Luc Van Lierde

I focused exclusively on long distances for two years (1997 and 1998, Author's note). When I returned to the world cup, on the short distance circuit, I noticed that training had changed enormously. After Japan, I decided to do multi-transitions on the advice of the Australians. For example: 15km warm-up followed by 3.5km very fast on the bike, together with 1km running, everything repeated five to six times. So the transition was five to six x (3.5km bike/1km run).

We did it in May 1999, but I think you have to start this type of work in January to be ready from March-April for the international circuit. The work has to be adapted, of course: shorter and less intense sessions in January with an increase in the number of transitions in the spring.

The type of transition has its limits. Training is not racing and if you multiply the intense sessions you get injured. People get injured more in training than in competition.

Philippe Martin

We practise transitions in training at special times of the year, especially within the framework of certain training camps organised in common.

We organise the camps in January (skiing and swimming in St Moritz) and at Easter (two weeks on the Costa Brava at sea level). The athletes are also in individual training camps in February/March.

We don't do any transitions in January. In the spring, in contrast, we suggest the following transition to be carried out several times: 200m swim, 1000m cycling, 200 to 400m run. The aim is to improve the technique and method of transitions (In the year of his first junior duathlon title in Glogow, Simone Aschwanden took more than a minute to get changed), but also to improve the physiological and biomechanical aspects of transitions (reducing the problem of inertia).

We also do simple transitions in all possible combinations: swimming-cycling, cycling-running, but also running-swimming, with the aim of optimising the phenomenon of adaptation.

We have also made it a habit to go for a run after each bike session, even a very short one (five minutes is enough).

As for the limits in transition training...I only see positive points! However, we should not do transitions all year round, mainly because that would end in boring the athletes.

Simon Lessing

I never do transitions. I've never done them. Because basically people are doing that as intensity work-outs, and I feel that what we should really be concentrating on is specific speed work which means that I'll prefer to go to a track and run 5x1000m, or a ladder, and focus on a specific speed work as opposed to go and do a brick. It is the same for the swim and the bike.

Triathlon is a strange sport: sensations are very different in swim, bike and run. It does not mean just because you are swimming bad that you are going to have a bad bike or a bad run. You are training in each and every single sport differently.

My transitions have improved. Generally speaking I am one of the fastest in the transition area. It is more a question of concentration than a question of practising. You have to concentrate one step at a time: put your bike down, undo your helmet, put your shoes on, etc. You have that sort of sequence, as opposed to going into the transition area just not thinking about what you are doing.

When you have done 200 triathlons in your life, that's good enough transition work.

Eduardo No Sanchez

We practise transitions to make everything that needs to be done automatic and fluid. We also use them to improve the run.

However, transitions are extremely tiring and pose a general recovery problem. This is why we don't do too many.

When we programme them we do them for example at day seven before the race, but never in the form of multi-transitions. Too tiring, in view of the current level of our athletes.

Susanne Nielsen

I do transitions, mainly with a view to long distance. I ride for three to four hours, for example, and run for an hour as soon as I get off the bike.

My coach thinks that too much intensity in cycling-running combinations can lead to injury. So he does not recommend transitions. According to him, transitions are more painful, the recovery longer and the legs more destroyed than when the sessions do not include transitions.

Cause or consequence? Competitions which include multiple transitions don't suit me.

Laurent Chopin

Transitions constitute the very essence of the triathlon. As such, they should be worked at in training, either in their simple form or in multi-transitions. As I have already underlined (see chapter: The Planning of Training), I suggest cycling-running transition sessions during the whole period of preparation, even if it's only a question on certain days of gentle jogging or doing a series of straights after a cycling session.

Transitions help to reproduce the conditions of fatigue found in competition (session of running at a certain pace on a base of pre-fatigue in cycling).

Finally, a point that I have not broached until the present moment. I am trying to set up what I call distance transitions. This consists, in the course of a week's planning, in placing the sessions in relation to each other so as to create a transition or deferred transitions.

For example, if the swimming and cycling sessions are programmed for Wednesday, and swimming and running Thursday, I position them in the following fashion: (Wednesday) swimming in the morning, cycling in the afternoon; (Thursday) running (track) in the morning, swimming (recovery) in the afternoon. That's how I reproduce, in a deferred transition, the order of triathlon events in competition.

Transitions are essential for the physiological and psychological preparation of triathletes. I see nothing wrong in doing them, save the difficulty in organising multi-transitions for an athlete without a squad and alone.

I'll give you an example of a training session combining cycling and running:

Cycling: relay work (groups of six cyclists) every 30 seconds (about every 300m) for three sets of 12 minutes (recovery 4min between each set). Instructions: maximise the distance covered, maintain group cohesion. Intensity: between threshold and maximum aerobic strength.

Running: ten minutes jogging, followed by a hill session broken down as follows: 8x(40sec at threshold uphill+4x20/20 at maximum aerobic velocity on the flat). Recovery jogging back down to the foot of the hill. Instructions: hills one to four alternating stride length and frequency, hills five to eight with a natural stride. Ten minutes active recovery followed by a long stretching session.

Finally, I programme some bike and run sessions. Once again, in a playful fashion. The athletes have a mountain bike between two or three of them and they combine ten to 15min running with 20 to 30min on the mountain bike. The repetitions can be themed.

The interest of this work lies in the transition, the time spent on it, as well as in the mutual support and organisation of the group.

CHAPTER EIGHT

STRENGTH TRAINING

The first thing about a triathlete's training is the large volume of it. Swimming, riding, running, takes time, lots of time, out of the day of someone smitten by the triple effort... a time which takes up other time: work time (not everyone is professional), meal times, social and personal time, sleep time...

This training also consumes a lot of energy and more than tires out the body. Between lengthy rides, track sessions and interminable series in the pool (50 metres!), they think of nothing else as night falls other than to fall into the arms of Morpheus!

So, how, in these already difficult conditions, is it possible to reconcile this voracious sport with all the other activities such as strength training, supposedly beneficial, but also likely to be counter productive, if you come out of it exhausted?

Triathletes and elite coaches position themselves as experts in this thorny subject, sometimes aggressively (that's why we love them) but never without a sledgehammer argument stemming from their long experience.

Strength training is a controversial subject in the triathlon world... without doubt, reading what follows. It is up to you to judge what can be got out of it.

Brett Sutton

'Musculation' is very big among sport scientists...

It took me three whole years to get rid of Loretta Harrop's muscles, accrued from many years of swimming, so that she could run fast. I have tried to do the same with Nancy Kemp-Arendt (from Luxembourg, she qualified as a swimmer for the 1988 Games in Seoul. She has based her international success in triathlon on a brilliant 1996, in the course of which she won the European cup, before finishing a magnificent tenth in the Sydney Olympics, Author's note).

Joanne King is skinny, frankly, and Jackie Gallagher is not exactly muscular, but both have exceptional international careers.

I am a big believer in musculation, in the sports for which it is necessary. I had a 50m freestyler in 22:05 and he did weights six times a week... However, my triathletes will do no weights unless they have a specific problem like Joanne King, who is very, very weak, or Jackie Gallagher who needs to resolve a specific problem in swimming.

As I said, we do strength work on the bike. I believe we do strength work also in the pool. We get by doing that. To paraphrase why, I think every kilo of extra muscle you put on is an extra 20 seconds slower you will run per 3km. It is no coincidence that Simon Lessing is most probably the leanest person in the sport, and we are going to see more Lessings and Van der Lindens in triathlon in the future (Eric Van der Linden, nicknamed the Flying Dutchman, represents a new generation of triathletes. Particularly at ease in the mountains, he has already won the Embrun and Schliersee triathlons. He distinguished himself in the 2000 European championships, leading the event until the final kilometre of the run when he was overtaken by England's Andrew Johns and the Swiss Reto Hug, Author's note).

I do not believe that swimmers need big muscles for 1500m. Most top guys are very slight. Kieren Perkins has never done weights. In Australia, distance swimmers don't lift anything. In triathlon, the bike is involved, but now drafting has destroyed the bike, so the strength condition is no more important.

If my athletes have a strength deficiency in swimming, we work obviously on the shoulder and the triceps. So we sort of isolate those particular muscles. We also do rhomboid work, very important and often neglected. That is where we get the shoulder problems. My swimmers do more than any others in triathlon, and we never had any shoulder problems.

In running, if somebody has a problem, we work on the hamstrings, and the calf and the Achilles tendon. These muscles are too underestimated in strength work because they play a considerable role in the prevention of injury, especially in swimmers.

Grégoire Millet

I don't propose strength training during the competitive period, simply because it is not at all convenient. But it does not shock me at all if certain athletes do it all year round.

I think of strength training in the following manner: maximum strength from the moment they restart training (for those experienced enough with heavy weights), followed very quickly with what I call repetitive strength training at 50 percent of maximum load (the athlete works with a weight that corresponds to 50 percent of the maximum load that he can lift in one go, Author's note). This should be done with a significant number of repetitions (50 to 60), in a circuit-training type of environment, with dynamic exercises (to repeat Gilles Cometti's terminology).

What's more, all of this should be done with an emphasis on co-ordination and balance at hyper-speed (as Jean-Pierre Egger suggests).

Chronologically, you first do general physical preparation to learn or relearn the drills; quickly we include repetitive strength; and finally you do the following standard series:

1) general strength exercise (for example, half squats);

2) a positional exercise (bounding for grouped jumps);

3) an exercise in hyper-speed, balance, co-ordination (sprint over 20m).

I consider the extensors of the lower body as the most important muscle group in triathlon: the whole quadriceps group, all the muscles which come into play when you stand on your toes. On the other hand I don't propose strength training for the upper body (biceps, triceps, upper back).

Because it is dynamic, strength training has a big aerobic impact, teaches posture and limits the force of resistance in the water and on land. I intervene, above all, in postural work. General physical preparation and circuit training let you work on posture, abdominals, co-ordination, and hyper-speed, with the help of plyometrics.

I am opposed to any strength training that alternates all types of muscular contractions within the same training session – we lack currently the valid experimental data in order to know the effects of alternating the different methods (included in Cometti's work, they should be regarded as hypotheses which have yet to be validated). The biggest problem of this approach is that you cannot master the limitations on time, which is catastrophic because in a process of preparation, one tries above all to control this type of data in order to be in form at the right moment.

Isabelle and Béatrice Mouthon

(Béatrice and Isabelle) General physical preparation comes first in our programme with a frequency of two sessions a week. When the period of specific strength training starts, we have one session a week of general physical preparation. Specific strength training (which includes heavy and repetitive work) is practised until the end of the winter period, and concentrates more on cycling. Work on the abdominals and gluteus is maintained throughout the whole year. Heavy strength work disappears progressively in the course of the pre-competitive period.

(Isabelle) I avoid doing strength training on Fridays so as not to have aches on Sunday. Lumbar, abdominal and gluteus work lasts some 30 minutes and always follows the same plan, no matter where we do it (including the lounge): we alternate, for example, 45 seconds supported on the elbows and the toes with the ankles extended or flexed, abdominals (for example 40 sit-ups) and a gluteus exercise (for example: on all fours, 30 elevations of each leg, straight out, in turn, and 30 leaps with the legs bent).

We do other exercises like: on your back, legs straight out, raise the pelvis 40 times. Leaning on an elbow, lateral exercise.

The same dynamic exercise with 30 scissors, 30 leg flexions, on each side, etc. Abdominals and lumbars are the most important muscle groups to work on, specifically to prevent pain because they are used throughout the whole of a triathlon: in swimming, to stay flat in the water; in cycling, to put pressure on the lumbar region so as to press down on the pedals; in running, to maintain the pelvic position and not let it collapse.

Recently we added aerobics in the gym to our programme which allows us to work on co-ordination, and to make training fun (in a group with music).

Karen Smyers

My body reacts violently to strength training. I have really sore muscles from it. I don't know whether I have an inconsistency with it or whether my body would finally adapt so that I would not be so sore if I did it for six months.

Anyway, I find that it affects my work-outs in running and biking and I have decided that it is better to have my specific work-outs go well than suffer. I am not positive that it is the right choice in the long-term but this is how I feel it right now.

I am already carrying a little bit more weight than ideal for an endurance event, and I am worried about getting too bulky.

On the other hand, I try to do specific strength training with e.g. the Vasa swim trainer which has helped me a lot. To build power on the bike, I prefer indoor training where I put my bike on a very, very hard gear and do eight times one minute of just a real power session rather than doing squats in the weight room.

Lothar Leder

Strength training is really important for general fitness. I don't do specific drills just for the swim or for the run. I jump from one machine to the other and do just how I feel. When I was with my gymnastics coach, I used to have specific drills, such as the stretch cord for the run.

I do strength training with a friend regularly twice a week in the winter time, starting in December and ending in March. When it gets warmer, I spend more time outside.

For me, lifting weights is a Saturday night thing, before you go out, or Sunday evening stuff if you're bored. I do it sometimes very late, like 10pm. Each session is one hour long, I do not work all muscle groups, that would be too much. I do stomach, back and legs for example, or just legs. I never do weights on two consecutive days. I do not really plan this conditioning in my swim-bike-run programme. It is just how it fits in. I do a lot of repetitions, for example 3x 25 to 30 reps, working on endurance rather than strength. With maximal strength work, you need a coach and you need to be careful. I am a big guy with heavy muscles already, and I do not want to build even more muscles.

Luc Van Lierde

I do strength training mainly in the winter. You can't dedicate only a month to it, but almost the whole year, three times a week, from one hour to one-and-a-quarter hours each time.

However, I stop completely two or three weeks before the competition season, because I need to rest after each race, and that does not go with strength training.

The exercises which I do in the gym, are based on a lot of endurance (six-week cycles), alternating from time to time with maximum strength (two weeks maximum). I use about a dozen exercises which cover all the muscle groups. The weights are light with a lot of reps.

I do not do any strength training outdoors.

Philippe Martin

I programme strength training the whole year round.

In the preparation phase we concentrate on strength endurance with, for example, two to three series of 30 reps at 40 percent max.

In the pre-competitive phase, we focus on exercises which develop explosiveness: five to six reps at 80 to 90 percent max.

Strength training is maintained for those athletes who lack strength. It is not on the programme, however, preceding a race, even though I am sure the athletes would benefit from it.

We do strength training in the gym but also outdoors: in swimming, for example, by means of paddles, weighted shoes and tee-shirt.

The main muscle groups targeted are: in swimming, the back; in cycling, the quads; in running, the rear leg group (calves and other extensors)

Strength training can be kept up throughout the whole year without risking accident. In contrast, it is worth paying attention to any drill which develops explosiveness.

Pure strength should only be done meticulously to serve as a reference point.

Simon Lessing

Strength training is something that is very individually athlete-orientated. There is not a given rule that all athletes should do specific gym work-outs. I have in the past done gym work-outs and I felt that was not necessary because it actually affected the way I felt training in terms of having tired legs, tired arms.

In fact, triathlon is a cross-training sport where you can benefit from doing specific strength work-outs on the bike or out in the run. The only things I have done in the past year or two is I have tried to work on specific areas where I have got problems, for example back problems or lower back problems. But for me, anyway, I know that I can do all the necessary strength programme during specific training.

And that's what I like about triathlon, that you have such a variation. In fact I go to the gym and do specific circuit training, just a general work-out focusing on abdominals and lower back, three times a week in the winter time, and twice a week in the summer time. Free-weight exercises, I don't push.

I do a fair amount of swimming with paddles on and I think it is a very, very good way of building up strength. I also think it is important to do other training work-outs when you are in a triathlon. You are always swimming in the wake or in the bubbles of somebody else and you lose that feel for the water. That's where paddles help: you are generally working on that feel through the water and it is also giving you a good strength work out to a certain extent.

Biking hills is great. This is what a couple of pro-cyclists have always said to me: if you can ride up a hill, you can ride anywhere.

I do no strength training in the run, because the work I do on the bike compensates for everything.

Eduardo No Sanchez

Strength training has two facets in our annual programming: technique in winter and feeling in the competitive period.

In fact, with the young athletes I only suggest strength training sessions for six to seven months, more depending on how mature the athletes are.

These sessions are only on the programme once every two weeks in the competitive period and if the season is very long I cancel them completely. Once again, I must stress what I understand by strength training: specific exercises, exclusively in swimming and cycling.

I pay particular attention to the shoulders insofar as the Spanish triathletes are not particularly good swimmers. In cycling, we have the chance of training the whole year thanks to the climatological conditions which the whole of Europe envies. This allows me to develop to the utmost my athletes' lower body strength.

Susanne Nielsen

I do a lot of strength training from November onwards each year. Three times a week for 12 weeks, then twice when the work intensifies. And when the competition season starts I stick to one session a week.

Each session lasts about an hour, but the circuits I do are longer (ten to 12 exercises) in winter than in the competitive period (six to seven exercises).

Laurent Chopin

I consider that strength training should be principally associated with technical proficiency: in swimming by having recourse to existing material (pull-buoy and paddles, elastic, etc.); in cycling, working with hard gears; in running, specific physical preparation and hill sessions.

Abdominals and the lumbar region should be worked on regularly, and throughout the whole year.

The athletes I coach, who have a physical therapist on call, do two strength sessions per week throughout the whole year.

The presence of a coach is vital to control technique. That's why strength training in the form of circuit training will never be programmed if the athletes are alone. What is more, this type of session is only beneficial from the moment the athlete possesses a sufficient technical level and has the time at his disposal. Clearly, these sessions are only reserved for the elite.

Triathlon is the association of three disciplines and training for it requires spending a lot of time training. Under these circumstances, devoting a specific amount of time to strength training might seem pointless, or counter-productive, since work on technical deficiencies should always take priority in training.

Triathlon is a complete sport in which all the muscle groups play an important role. So it is important to take care of their harmonious development.

Well conducted strength training helps you maintain quality technical proficiency for a long time. At the same time it lets you realign or compensate for weak musculature. But this investment in time is not always justified taking into account the many demands of the discipline. So it is always your aims which will decide training priorities.

CHAPTER NINE

NUTRITION

The best and only rule is to pay attention to what you eat throughout the whole year, not only the day before a race, or the week before a major objective. Luc Van Lierde

Food, nutrition, dietetics… very often a nightmare for us French. Bon vivants that we are, we have to force ourselves to banish dishes with rich sauces, fine wines, cakes and other sweets which abound in our country and which make France the envy of the world…

That's the problem: we are triathletes as well, condemned mostly to solitary effort and an abyss of calories for an increasingly fragile motor as the racing season approaches.

It is a cruel dilemma! Does everything have to stop, at the risk of losing the taste for life and getting depressed, or do you pretend that nothing is happening, and wait to be mown down by some illness (there are those among us who have the secret to this), in the heat of battle? What rules do you follow (if possible, simple ones) in order not to jeopardise your health? What food do you take before, during and after a race?

This chapter is a real feast for the eyes as much as the taste buds. How healthy these athletes are!

Brett Sutton

I have seen Olympic gold medallists eating nothing but McDonald's. I tell my athletes: "If you are racing well, and if you are happy with what you are eating, keep eating it". Why upset the mentality?

I try to advise and treat my athletes as adults. Nutrition is one part of the whole picture and I totally believe it is an invisible training aid, which is good, but I put the priority where I think it should be. And the priority may be stretching, or pelvic stability, or the psychology of what happens if you get beaten, and all that comes before the meal! I am a very simple person, and I like to look at the main dish first and look at the dessert later. I may find that the dessert is overtaking the meat and potatoes in a lot of areas.

In Australia, I am always fighting because I like my athletes to have a certain amount of fat, but there you must have loads of carbohydrate and low fat and low protein. When I come to Europe, there is a certain amount of fat in the diet and everybody is happy, and nobody is sick, and the athletes go well, the new system seems to go very well over here, and so I go back home and say: well I believe we should have a bit of fat in the diet. They just laugh!

If you are training five or six hours a day, you are a fat burner. In Australia, my people say: "Well, the research says..." I don't care about the research, the fact is: five hours a day, at 60 to 70 percent of their max, they are fat-burning machines.

Before a race my athletes will eat what is comfortable for them, but they will build up carbohydrate two days before the race. So the main meal for a race comes two days earlier, because I do not take glycogen out of them the day before with training. So I would like to make sure that glycogen is loaded up, and that they don't have to over-eat the day before a race.

A pizza is an example of what is on the menu for dinner the day before a race and everyone is happy about that. The day of the race they'll get up and have some bread with jam, or something like that. Nothing more if the race is early, but some carbohydrate if the race is later on, so as not to race on an empty stomach. In the French races that are staged on Sunday afternoon, they have a good carbohydrate meal on Saturday evening. Not a big one, but a good one.

Then, on any particular day, I like their breakfast to be carbohydrate meals as well. And they can add a sort of snack during the day if they wish. It is very important that they do understand that that can help.

During and after a race I get back to water as being the most important intake (in short distance races). I tried the energy bars, but that stuff is killing them. It dehydrates them terribly.

So we try not to drink any gassy drink 72 hours beforehand. If they travel, they have got to have a bottle of water with them, and I like them to sort of overcompensate rather than undercompensate, because I believe one of the big problems in triathlon is water intake.

I have verified it. On the run for instance, it is a quarter of a cup, if you actually measure what goes down. So they must drink a bit of water on the bike. My juniors would say: "I felt good, so I did not want to drink", and then they die during the run... So now I check the bottles after the races.

Of course the approach for Nice, Hawaii, or Zofingen would be totally different. Greg (Welch) used Gatorpro and started drinking that four hours before the race, then straight out of the swim, then we try every hour to replenish the carbohydrate and triglycerol. And then he would eat whatever bar he was sponsored by, as a snack each hour. I'd be very disappointed if he did not have something within each particular hour. He'd have another bottle by the halfway mark on the bike, with a carbohydrate drink.

I think the Dissociated Scandinavian Regimen must be good theoretically, but it causes them other troubles because their bodies are not used to it, so you're giving them another stress. I try to replenish their glycogen stores, rather than overload them.

Grégoire Millet

I am not an expert in nutrition. I refer to specialists like Denis Riché (a sports nutritionist who takes care of many elite athletes in a wide number of disciplines,

Author's note). I prefer the athletes to stick to something worked out by them, than that they should keep trotting out some well-known rules that they all know anyway.

My only hobby-horse in nutrition is fatty acid balance. The athletes who have digestive, muscular and tendon problems or who recover badly are often those athletes who eat spicy foods. In a heavy training period or a lactic period, I give them lists of foods which are acidic or acidifiers.

If I have to advocate a final meal before competition, I opt for simple things like pasta with chicken and salad. I am very careful about hydration. I insist that all my athletes carry their water bottle with them always.

For me, the ideal thing is to eat when you are out on the bike for more than an hour. Solids should be taken and glucose drinks, because it is of paramount importance to maintain glycogen levels.

Before a race I advocate a drink (no solids) containing fructose, which has the advantage of not producing an insulin reaction. During a race: in a race like Hawaii the Mouthon sisters dilute their products as they go along, so they do not have to take what the organisation offers. That, then, poses problems of concentration. The girls have powder and make their own mixture themselves. I don't push eating solids, apart from bananas, maybe. I think what is taken in a race should essentially be liquid.

Post-race, the ideal situation is to consume foods with a high glycogen content, as well as amino acids. I recommend bicarbonated drinks as soon as possible after the end of a race. In general, I always tell my athletes that any increase in weight affects performance.

An anecdote? I recall signing a contract with an elite athlete, stating that if she did not lose X amount of weight in the first four months of our coach-athlete relationship, I would disassociate myself from all responsibility with regard to the objectives I had committed myself to with her.

I support the Dissociated Scandinavian Regimen, at least with those athletes who want to use it. I have tested it on myself and it has always given good results. Some of my athletes have tried it with success so I see no objection to this regimen, at least where long distances are concerned. When I tested this on myself, I opted for a reduced format: Tuesday and Wednesday low carbohydrate content (the regime was not only fats and proteins); Thursday, Friday, Saturday high carbohydrate content. The Mouthon sisters, for example, follow the extreme formula.

Isabelle and Béatrice Mouthon

(Isabelle) I eat a little of everything but without excess. A balanced diet, fat-reduced, with limited refined foods (white bread, white pasta) and no industrial products such as mayonnaise. I try to eat a lot of vegetables and wholemeal bread. I make my own bread and jam myself to avoid anti-oxidants and all the other unconventional products which find their way into foodstuffs.

(Béatrice) Above all, I avoid animal fats in favour of vegetable fats because it is necessary. I favour vegetables over starchy foods which I don't eat much of apart from bread. I am not really fond of noodles or spaghetti. I like white meat which I eat in moderation.

The idea of rationing food or following a strict regime must be banned in sport. It is the best way of avoiding health problems. Food must continue to be consumed while training. When you go out for a bike ride for example you must always have fructose in the water bottle. This will help against health problems and infection.

We don't have a typical meal, but we have certain combinations and follow our own ideas. We eat typical breakfasts. At midday we don't eat proteins (because they're difficult to digest and won't be assimilated in time for the afternoon session) and we combine starchy foods and green vegetables. We keep the protein, with vegetables and mixed salads, for the evening. In brief: proteins in the evening and carbohydrates at midday, with milk products taken three or four times throughout the day.

The last meal before competition: we have a habit of eating half an Equilibral (Overstim) three hours before a race which helps us survive. We find it works together with a cup of tea. For the long distances, where the start is often very early in the morning, we eat our cake a little later (up to one-and-a-half hours before the start). If the race does not start until late in the afternoon, the day starts with breakfast: white bread, compote, sometimes yoghurt (because some protein is necessary). It is better to avoid fibre, refined sugar, and above all fruit juices.

While waiting for the start, we have a habit (on the advice of Denis Riché) of taking 10g of fructose with 500 or 750ml of water, to be drunk at regular intervals during the hour before the race.

(Isabelle) Even if a race lasts only two hours, I find it wrong not to take anything apart from water. Even if you feel as though there is no need during the race, it helps post-race recovery. In cycling we take a bottle of at least 750ml, sometimes two, according to race conditions, which we dilute, more or less depending on the external temperature, with dietetic products (we have opted for Hydralixir of Overstim). But we take a lesser dose than recommended. Running, I take 20cl of concentrated glucose at the fifth kilometre, as well as all the recommended nutrients (we don't leave anything out), paying particular attention to the proposed drinks.

(Béatrice) In general, we only drink water in the run, and baulk at taking on board a drink that we have not suitably tried and tested.

Over long distances we take solids about every 40 kilometres in cycling, and try to take on board proteins and fats. To the extent that we find long distances difficult, we have turned towards liquid foods which allow us to drink 'solid'. A piece of advice, however: it is absolutely vital to train for taking food and digesting it while competing. It is something that our bodies are not prepared for. And one product can suit one person and not another. So testing different products during long distance training is a personal approach.

Post-race, we hydrate ourselves, we drink Cola-Cola and eat yoghurt which is really welcome an hour after a race, as well as bananas and water melon. Later we favour savoury over sweet: nourishing lentils and vegetable protein.

After a long distance race, we hate PowerBars. Honestly, I can no longer stand carbohydrate. We dream of a nice glass of beer and are ready for all sorts of excess after so many privations. We let ourselves go!

An anecdote? In Hawaii the water given to the competitors is completely demineralised. As good Frenchwomen we are used to our water being packed with minerals, which means that both of us have had enormous problems in digesting this water which lies on our stomachs. So we allow for salty, bicarbonated solutions for improved assimilation.

For long distance triathlons, our specific dietary approach begins one week before the race in the form of the Dissociated Scandinavian Regimen. This regime is contentious, but it suits us and is a real psychological motivation. Into the fifth hour of a race (this applies to Nice as well as Hawaii) the Dissociated Scandinavian Regimen is a profitable procedure. We begin the Sunday before the race with training or competition during which we do not take carbohydrate or when we have finished. Monday, Tuesday and Wednesday we apply the lipid protein principle (with however 20 percent carbohydrate) while continuing to train in order to deplete our carbohydrate reserves. Wednesday is the hardest day from a mental point of view: we become aggressive, we have no energy, we go training with the feeling that we are fasting even though we have eaten… So you have to be strong mentally and tell yourself that you will get the return the following Sunday. From Thursday on it is resurrection time. From the moment we take the least amount of sugar, we feel our strength returning and our batteries are recharged. Then we slow down our training which is light. Thursday and Friday are carbohydrate loaded and on Saturday we eat a little of everything above all for the last meal.

Dietary side-effects? In winter, during our month's rest, we put on a nice little adipose tissue (3kg+ on our bodyweight) which motivates us to start training again!

When you really desire something it is often because you are frustrated or lack something emotionally. Personally, when my head is together, I don't feel the need for anything. Recently, I was with some people who threw themselves on some Brownies and offered me some. I took some, more to please them than for pure pleasure (even though they were really good). In truth, a real pleasure for me when it is hot is a beer.

(Isabelle) And for me a Coke! And now that people organise pasta parties, I shall organise pizza parties!

There are some athletes who are crazy about food and others for whom it is not a priority, like Greg Welch, or Paula Newby Fraser who was eating entire packets of sweets just before Nice, something which really upset me, because I was young and thought she was taking her job really seriously.

I remember travelling with Miles Stewart and his father. Miles is the prototype Australian beef eater… And wherever he was he had to have his steak and chips midday or evening, even in Japan where meat is unobtainable. That has always had an effect on me. Besides, he is a beautiful baby!

Karen Smyers

My basic rule of thumb is to try and get balanced meals as consistently as possible with proteins, carbohydrates and fat in every meal, with a focus on higher carbohydrates and not overdoing the fats.

I look for variety in food, I listen to my body when it screams for a steak for example! I will have red meat twice a week. I keep an eye on my weight, since in the winter time I tend to put on a few extra pounds. So in the springtime I try to watch a little bit what I am eating, and cut down on beer (I am a beer drinker; it is one of my indulgences!) I am not really strict on this, and I guess it keeps me mentally happy in the long term. If triathlon required me to cut off beer out of my diet and never have a dessert I would probably not stay in the sport in the long term!

I do not agree with the Dissociated Scandinavian Regimen.

During Ironman training, I might add a recovery drink to my daily intake (that includes many vitamins).

The night before an Ironman, I stick to something that I am comfortable with like a pasta meal with red sauce, which digests pretty quick and will not come and haunt me the next day.

If a race is in the afternoon, I also like oatmeal for breakfast since it is high carbohydrate and is pretty quickly digested. I also like a banana.

During Hawaii, I have usually relied on the carbohydrates offered there. I have actually not found something that I love yet.

A funny story? When Saint Croix was a long (4 to $4^1/_2$ hour) race (dream race in the Virgin Isles, Author's note), I remember taking a PowerBar with me (I had never had one before). I was riding along with Colleen Cannon and I took one bite, which I chewed for about five minutes before spitting it out and telling her: "How can people eat these things?!" I don't enjoy having anything solid while I am breathing. It is incompatible to chew and breathe at the same time! I prefer to digest a liquid, too. Bananas are OK, because they do not involve too much chewing.

Lothar Leder

Three weeks before an Ironman, I try to avoid chocolate and all the bad stuff: too much sugar and fat, Coke! I am genetically programmed to be obese (my dad weighs 130 kg), and when I stop after Hawaii I get big very quickly. Nicole is a great help here: eat this, do not eat that! I tried to work with nutritionists, but they are very complicated… In my everyday life, I have no rule as regards food. I eat whatever I want when I want. But if I run a fast 30km for example, I have to eat immediately afterwards, for recovery: pasta or anything solid.

On race day I eat the normal breakfast I have in my everyday life: toast and coffee. A lot of people eat, for example, a PowerBar on race day and then they are surprised to encounter problems during the race...

I have become addicted to coffee: I can go training only if I have a coffee before! Even worse, if I think I'll have a fast interval session, I need to drink three cups of coffee. One of my hobbies besides cars is sitting in coffee shops!

In triathlon, a lot of people are too extreme. When I was a junior, I was vegetarian for three years. I had read it in a book and I wanted to be cool, so I did it. One day I said to my mum: I am not going to eat meat anymore. She dealt with it... The thing is that when I stopped being a vegetarian my running times started to improve immediately in the weeks afterwards.

I eat meat three times per week. My father is a hunter, so I eat of lot of wild meat. It is non-fat and really healthy meat. In the training period, I like to eat Kaiserschmarrn: it is a speciality from Vienna and Bavaria. It is a sweet scrambled pancake, that you can make very quickly, and it is very a good carbo after bike or run. It gives you full energy for the next training sequence. They serve it at the ETU cup Schliersee (Schliersee is on the Bavarian/Austrian border, Author's note) on the finish line, with apple compote. Mmmmhhhhh!

How can Joanne King eat two chocolate bars before starting an Ironman? How? I tell you: I thought about trying it too. Serious!

If the race is in the afternoon, I will eat whatever is available at the hotel or with my team. I don't care. I only try to avoid meat on race day. Too heavy. I stick to carbo.

One or two hours before a long distance race, I may eat a PowerBar or bananas. I take nothing during short races. I just drink a lot. This is crucial. Plain water is the best.

Long course : 90 percent carbo during bike and run, and Coke during the run. In Hawaii, I eat a PowerGel every 5km on the run, starting at km 20. I figured that out when trying it during training. For four years, I ate nothing during the whole Ironman. It sounds strange. I just had carbo-drinks. In fact, I had problems: every time I ate something, I threw up. Today, I have forced myself and convinced my body to eat. And it works.

After a short race, I am very hungry. If I have a race the next week-end, I have a high carbo-drink (mixed already) in the half-hour following the finish, to recover.

After a long course, I am not hungry. I eat at night, I go for salty things like French fries. And all the shit you cannot eat before the race. Now that the big race is over, your mind wants to eat that crazy stuff.

My food pleasures? Cream ! Mixed cream on cakes, whipped cream. But it is really dangerous... And chocolate bars when I go to gas stations. And Coke! It really got very bad in the last years: in the morning, Coke; every time I go to the gas station, Coke; in training, Coke; after training, Coke...

I have never tried the Dissociated Scandinavian Regimen. Apparently it worked very well for Thomas Hellriegel, and Rainer Mueller. I have never tried it because I never knew how to do it exactly. I should maybe try it.

I see a lot of food at finish line. My food, which I throw up! In fact, if it came to a sprint finish, I can push my limits until I throw up. Like at the world cup Tiszaujvaros (Hungary) against Dmitry Gaag (from Kazakhstan he became world champion in Montreal 1999, beating Simon Lessing, Author's note). It only happens on the short course, and sometimes even before I finish.

I have had good experiences with Red Bull (high in caffeine), on the bike.

Luc Van Lierde

The best and only rule is to pay attention to what you eat throughout the whole year, not only the day before a race, or the week before a major objective.

I am not obsessed with nutrition. If I like something I eat it, even if it is not particularly recommended. But I eat it in small quantities. The important thing is to take care over 12 months.

When I prepare for long distance, I weigh 68 to 69kg. In winter, I allow myself three kilos more than in the summer. I cannot put on six or seven kilos in winter because that would be too hard and would cost me too much energy to get it off afterwards.

There is not a dish that I particularly like, any more than there is a dish I completely dislike.

When I am overweight, I eat only fruit in the morning and no protein in the evening because digestion takes too long and I don't sleep well. Protein takes at least eight hours to be digested and that disturbs my sleep and therefore my recovery. I don't eat much meat. If I eat it, it is white meat or fish.

In the three days that precede a competition I eat a lot of pasta which I take with some meat, but no vegetables. I do not combine the three. I eat three hours to three hours 30 minutes before each race and I eat well. It does not give me any problem. Then, I drink about a litre of carbohydrate before the start.

During a short distance race, just as in a long distance race, I take a carbohydrate drink. It is my nectar. During the short, I don't eat. In contrast, for the long distance I force myself to consume dry food during the cycling (for example an energy bar) every 30 minutes, so that my stomach does not make me suffer. It is, in fact, the only reason I have for eating during a triathlon. And if I have the same problem during the run, I eat bananas. Generally, in a long distance triathlon, I take carbohydrate in the run.

After a race, I have protein as soon as possible, for example a milk shake.

I like to have a beer with my physiotherapist after a session each week.

I have been practising a form of Dissociated Scandinavian Regimen for years before each race, long as well as short. In fact I concentrate on protein at the beginning of the week and the carbohydrates from Thursday on.

As for energy products, I use Twinlap which has an extensive range of products.

Philippe Martin

Firstly, nutritional balance seems to me absolutely vital. The athlete must be aware of what he eats. Eat a lot of carbohydrates. In Switzerland we are trying new products based on fats for example.

Some years ago, Olivier Bernhard (Swiss world class duathlete, won the legendary Zofingen Powerman in Switzerland several times, Author's note) wrung his spaghetti in a towel to get rid of the oil. The following year he took the oil bottle and swamped his pasta with it.

Rules? No rule, apart from not eating fondue before a race! However, if an athlete is convinced it is good for him you won't be able to convince him to the contrary. That said, if my athletes want to eat fast food the day before an important race, it makes me nervous.

It is difficult to control an athlete's diet when you are travelling abroad (I have some memories of the Cancun world championships…). It is however not so important a long time before a race. Only the final meals are of paramount importance.

Finally, my big rule would be to respect the eating habits of the athletes.

Fifteen minutes before starting a race I recommend drinking 20 to 30cl of plain water. After the race, you have to take carbohydrates with water in the 20 minutes after you finish. It is necessary to fill up the reservoir again.

I believe in the Dissociated Scandinavian Regimen, like a lot of Swiss athletes, as much for the short distance as the long. We use PowerBar bars and Spozer drinks. I don't believe in the effects claimed for Red Bull.

Simon Lessing

There are many athletes who are too concerned about what they eat. I am not a vegetarian, I eat meat. I think the basic rule is to have a healthy diet, which means not going eating at McDonald's every two days. I eat a lot of salads, a lot of rice, potatoes, pastas (lasagna is my favourite dish). Of course, because of what our sport demands, you need to eat carbohydrates. But you know, after a good day of training, I do not mind some cake or some ice-cream. I am pretty relaxed, and I think it is important because the training is so hard for triathlon that if you make your eating regime so hard as well, mentally it is just too tough. You got to have a few enjoyments. Look at me: I eat relatively large amounts of food and I am quite skinny.

I usually have two to three cups of coffee a day. I like a cup of coffee before I go running in the morning. It helps me wake up, it gives me a kick.

If I race at midday or in the afternoon my last meal will be the breakfast. If I race in the morning, I try to wake up at least three hours before the start and have a couple of pieces of toast. I like to race on an empty stomach, or relatively empty stomach. I can't keep down my food if I train or race on a full stomach... I feel terrible. In any case since I am specialised in short distance racing, I don't really need to worry too much.

I usually don't feel like eating after a race. If it is really hot, I like to drink. I don't know how athletes can eat lots of cakes straight after a race. I just don't have the appetite for that.

Concerning the Scandinavian Dissociated Regimen, I don't think you should deprive your body of certain elements that you need during training and preparation for a race. You should try to be concentrating on trying to keep everything as normal as possible and not to stress the body out. The race is hard enough as it is.

When I prepared for Nice, I had no specific diet. The problem I had in Nice the first time I raced there was that I was so nervous that I vomited all my breakfast, so I started Nice, when I raced against Mark (Allen), on a completely empty stomach. I did not eat any solids on the bike, I just had a squeezy carbohydrate, and I completely ran out of energy on the run. So the second year I did Nice, I tried to eat solids and definitely felt that was much better. With a little bit of solids and some carbohydrate drink, that was enough for me.

I experimented quite a lot during training because, obviously coming from the short distance, I did not have a lot of endurance, my metabolism was very, very high, and after two hours on the bike, I was very hungry while other athletes who'd been racing longer distance for a longer time could go out for four or five hours without eating anything. So I had to train my body to lower my metabolism.

I like to drink a product made by Leppin called 'Daily Training Formula'. It is a multi-mineral, amino-acid and multi vitamin drink that I have used now for many years, especially when the weather is very hot like in the South of France and you are sweating a lot every day.

I have never been anaemic. In the summer when it is very hot you lose your appetite and don't feel like eating a big bowl of pasta. So I generally make myself a smoothy, mixing fruits (apples, bananas) and carbohydrate powder. It is a very good meal, easy to prepare and to drink or eat.

Eduardo No Sanchez

When we mention questions concerning diet in triathlon, I think immediately of two things: health... and body weight. I try to place at my athletes' disposition a maximum of information about how to feed oneself efficiently and to the best extent: specialist articles, reference works...

A triathlon licence... from 1927!

Luc Van Lierde, at the European championships in Madeira (Portugal)

Waiting for the start in Vuokatti (Finland)

Making a splash in Madeira

Orientating oneself while swimming

The buoy gets a battering at the Perth world championships

Beating the waves at Haïfa (Israel)

The Australian Loretta Harrop, programmed to win

The German Dirk Bockel, on the way towards glory at the European Cup

Transition time for Simon Lessing in Australia

European cycle courses can be hard

No seconds to lose at the finish of the bike ride

Karen Smyers, superstar of the triathlon

Triathlète magazine

"I planned my objectives according to my dreams." Isabelle Mouthon in Sydney

'Sir' Simon, multiple world champion, winning at Cancun (Mexico).

Triathlète magazine

Isabelle and Béatrice Mouthon, the inseparable triathlon twins

Stefan Vuckovic, Sydney Olympic silver medallist, shows how hard it was

Susanne Nielsen at Velden (Austria)

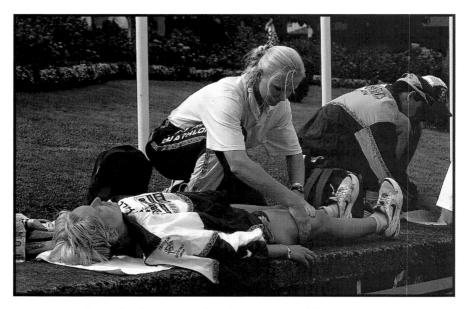

The South Africans at work at the Guernica world championships

The 1999 European Championships: J. Rehula (2nd), R. Hug (1st), M Krnavek (3rd)

Olivier Marceau, world champion in 2000, seventh at the Sydney Olympics

Classically, the last true meal (dinner) before a race consists of slow release carbohydrate. For breakfast our culture inclines towards bread, butter or margarine and honey. To that we add rice or pasta.

During the race, Spanish athletes most often take with them two very different bottles (not necessarily full): one with water, the other with a glucose saline solution. They also take Powergel which they use or not depending on the course, the climatological conditions, if they are alone or in a group, etc. Finally, for long distances, they feed on solid food like pancakes, rice pudding, energy bars, etc.

We experience a lot of difficulty here in Spain with our athletes who do all sorts of things after a race and we notice a number of tendencies approaching bulimia (chocolate and sweets, among others) or anorexia.

Concerning the Dissociated Scandinavian Regimen, I have used it seven or eight times, but I find that the gains are very slight considering the sacrifices needed to follow it properly. What is more, to get any benefit from it, the athlete needs the perfect psychological and physiological balance right from the start.

Susanne Nielsen

I don't eat that much chocolate (laughs)! There's too much fat in chocolate. On the other hand, I eat sweets and chewing gum, because I use the sugars they contain.

Among my working rules, I eat meat three or four times a week. So I am not vegetarian and consider protein extremely important for the body. In contrast, I don't eat pork or red meat, unless it is well cooked. If not my stomach suffers for two whole days.

My last meal before a race? Pasta without meat. I eat after every race, even if I have to force myself! If I want to eat something, I do it without remorse. At any moment of the year. And that includes chocolate! I also drink alcohol: cocktails, champagne, etc. But I don't like it enough to get drunk. Obviously, I don't drink when I'm peaking or have peaked. After… no problem! That said, when I am preparing for a goal, even though I know that a little wine is good for health, I decide against straying from the straight and narrow.

An anecdote that could have had dramatic results for me: during the 1996 European championships in Hungary, I was not able to eat at all for the first two days. The local food, based on potatoes in gravy with meat was simply awful (Susanne became European champion that year, Author's note).

Laurent Chopin

My main rules concerning food are general ones for endurance athletes. They are well known. I don't have a special recipe.

When a problem arises I have a specialist treat my athletes. The coach should not be the only one to be involved in the preparation of an elite athlete. I think of things more in team terms and the nutritionist should be part of that.

Athletes have to be educated in nutrition, in order to avoid mistakes prejudicial to their performance. My elite athletes are all, or almost all, contracted with sports dietary brands which in itself constitutes a guarantee in this area.

I don't advocate any particular meal, I simply respect the main rules of sports nutrition. The last meals before competition should be rich in fuel: carbohydrates. The athlete should also make sure he drinks enough water. For the final meal my athletes often eat special cake like Overstim.

When a competition is on the afternoon – let's say 14.00hrs – they have breakfast at 8am: tea, fruit juice, bread and butter with honey, yoghurt; three hours before the race they have the cake. If the race is in the morning, the cake will be eaten three hours before the start.

The last meal is not, in fact, the most important. It is all the meals from the last three days which are important. During the race, each athlete has his usual drink. Not all triathletes absorb the same drink in the same way. Their bodies respond differently. Each athlete knows what suits him from experience. But generally, they use drinks that can easily be found in the shops, of the No 4 type.

For training, the only little recipe that I advocate is the mixture of fruit syrup in a 75cl bottle with a pinch of salt.

During a short triathlon, liquid food is enough. In a long distance race, on the other hand, it is better to alternate solids and liquids at regular intervals. Only experience can, in fact, say what suits an athlete. In any case, it is important to be vigilant during the ride because a good run is decided on the bike. So: solid and liquid in the ride! As for the run, it may be difficult for some to assimilate solids. So Coke might be a good substitute.

As for post-race nutrition, the first thing is to rehydrate, above all with carbonated water, to eliminate acidity. You have to avoid heavy foods (red meat, fats…). It is important to think about restoring energy stocks.

Food fads? In nutritional matters I don't give my athletes orders. They're big enough to decide for themselves what they eat. I keep to my role as adviser, with more or less influence depending on the individual. If an athlete really wants something it is because their body demands it, so I cannot object. But it is important that the fad does not become an aberration, nor that is should be indulged in too often. But the third half* is part of the game. It de-stresses.

In principle, the theory behind the Dissociated Scandinavian Regimen is interesting. In practice, I refuse to play sorcerer's apprentice.

*the third half is a term from the game of rugby. The game consists of two halves and the third half is the eating and drinking after the game!

CHAPTER TEN

_____

HILL TRAINING

I definitely think that cycling hills helped my strength on the run. Simon Lessing.

Hill training, in cycling and running, has a number of advantages and drawbacks. On the positive side is physical condition, power, technique, speed and development of energy potential… On the minus side are the specific sessions which require… a hill near you, the desire to do them and make yourself suffer, to know how to use them so that the effects obtained at the end of the planned sessions are not the opposite of what was intended…

When and how to plan a hill session in cycling and running? What type of hill do you choose for a certain objective? What are the effects? What pitfalls are to be avoided? And the descent? The answers to these questions show, for once, a certain unity among the experts, triathletes and coaches.

Something to reassure modest practitioners such as us!

Brett Sutton

We do hills at least once a week. At the moment, we are doing a hill which is 1.7km, and we sit in the saddle for that. On another hill right next to it we've got 1.1 km and we get off the saddle for that. One is a three minute hill, and the other is a five minute hill. We get out of the saddle on the steep hill, so they practise their technique. This is why my guys do well on hilly courses.

Hills give power and reduce injury. I think it is important that they ride bigger gears. I don't try to teach my people to spin. I let the cyclists do that. I want them ready for the run. Greg Bennett, Craig Walton, Ben Bright are able to jump off in front. And when they sit in the pack, they don't spin (they never go faster than 80rpm maximum, Author's note), neither Simon or the other guys. They do a lot less spinning and push bigger gears. Ben used to be 64rpm when he was a kid, and we are around 80 with him now but we won't go any faster.

If there is a hill in the race that we are preparing, we actually incorporate hills in our training programme. The goal is to attack on the hill, that's basically the game plan. So we'll be working on one hill on the bike in the six weeks preceding the world championships.

The Perth course contained a hill, and was done five times. That hurt. We had worked on that particular type of hill... But this was nothing comparable to Lausanne 1998, where the type of people who were to do well could only be climbers. I put in a report to Triathlon Australia that the athletes who did well in Perth on a flat course might

137

not be the people that we should have in Lausanne. This is why I was supporting Benjamin (Bright) who is a superior climber, and I wanted to test Greg Bennett and Chris McCormack in Embrun, where they did wonderfully. For the women it was not so critical. Jackie has the technical skills do go down, but Emma can't descend. That was the biggest worry with the girls: I said: "The girls who can descend are the girls who will win". You may make 20 seconds going up and lose 1.30 on the downhill... Therefore we had to come to Switzerland for three months and practise. And it is on the descent that Joanne King became world champion that year....At the top of each hill she was dropped, but she came back on each descent, thanks to a 53/11 which nobody had noticed before the race.

Concerning running, I repeat again and again: first put in place the technique, only then can you put into practice other aspects of running, like hills.

Injuries indicate the limit of hill training in both cycling and running. There are knee injuries in cycling when the athletes don't have the minimum mileage necessary (which all the cyclists have). Triathletes don't ride 1000km a week. If my kids had the leisure to ride twice a day for the next six years, then, yes: they would become kings of spin. They don't have that opportunity...so I compromise as ever: we have the strength necessary for the big gears which need less recourse to specific motor skills…

Grégoire Millet

I use hills in the training programmes of the athletes I train both in winter and the competitive period.

Hill running is interesting for technique. What is more, I think (rightly or wrongly) that the injuries associated with running should occur less on hills, because the shock wave when you put the foot down is not as great.

I like to regard hill running as strength training (by using bounding, for example). Every now and then I also like to suggest a fast interval hill session. A typical session might be: warm-up; six minutes of 30/30 on the hill; the same on the flat; the same descending. Endless variations on this session are obviously possible.

On the other hand, I do not make the athletes do sessions aimed properly speaking at developing metabolic power. I do not want to make them do three minute all-out sessions.

In cycling, I use the hills for strength training, in the saddle or off it, on big gears, even though that creates a lot of tension on the ligaments. I also like interval work where the intervals oscillate between one and two kilometres, six or eight times, with a two-minute recovery.

Whether cycling or running, you should never hesitate to work on a hill to prepare specifically for certain races where hills have an important place in the race profile. For example, the year Isabelle prepared for Zofingen we did a lot of hill work. Unfortunately we did not pay as much attention to the descent…

The hills let you do lactic or maximum aerobic power work more easily. Hills have a certain cardiovascular impact, but you cannot say that this is directly beneficial for cycling on the flat inasmuch as the muscle groups are not engaged in the same way.

There are certainly limits but in my opinion there are no drawbacks to using hills in training. Even in running, there can be a strong cardiovascular effect that does not necessarily lead to the mechanical limitations experienced on the flat (the speed being less).

Isabelle and Béatrice Mouthon

In cycling, we do hills for strength training. But also to prepare for certain events like for example the 1998 world championships in Lausanne for which we had trained intensively and specifically.

There is a hill near our house which extends for 12 kilometres with a gentle rise that is relatively constant (five to six percent). We climb it in the saddle with the aim of changing down one tooth for each kilometre we ascend while maintaining the same speed. So our cadence is around 90rpm at the beginning and finishes on 50. The aim is muscular not physiological (the heart rate does not exceed 155bpm). Raising the gear by one tooth at regular intervals lets us get into the session progressively without putting too much pressure on the joints. Only the thighs work, we refine our pedal technique, and we try not to pull too much on the handlebars (to do this we try to hold the handlebar with only one finger).

In running, even though we do regular hill work, we have noticed that we need to organise this type of session in the future.

In the course of the winter we do a hill session every week with our athletics club in Aix. The hill intervals do not last more than a minute on a gradient no steeper than ten percent. A typical session might consist of three series of six hills, recovering on the descent, with five minutes between each series. We do work on stride and cadence, finishing, for example, by practising hyper-speed or by progressively increasing the speed. In general, we finish these sessions at maximum pulse rate, which corresponds to the aim of developing maximum aerobic power. In addition to this physiological aim this type of session gives you a better quality stride and is good strength training which you later feel the benefit of on the flat.

Like all good things, it is better not to indulge this too much. If the hills are too long or the number of reps too high, you run the risk of fatigue and overtraining.

Karen Smyers

Particularly in biking, hills are a great way to get in shape, specifically for strength and power. You can really get your heart rate elevated for a long period of time. Good threshold training. Almost all of my bike courses include hills and have hours worth of climbing in them. This is one of my favorite work-outs.

I bike hills almost all year round, and I adapt my gearing to the goals. There are days especially when it comes to the beginning of the season where I go as hard as I can for one to three minutes and I record my time between two specific points. I do vary my gears, climb sitting or standing, use different hill courses with gentle or steeper climbs.

I do a hard hill session once every two weeks and it includes a total of 20 minutes of hard work altogether.

I don't do as much hill work in running. I do part of the Boston marathon course where there is a grassy section that runs up the hill, which my running club has marked off every 200m. A particular session that we often do is up 200 (down) up 400 (down) up 600 (down) up 800 (down), and we record the time for the entire session.

Lothar Leder

Hills really helped me in running. I was living in a flat area before, in the Rhine Valley. Now I am close to Frankfurt, and I have improved my running because I have to run uphill everyday. I have a slight 5km uphill systematically included in my running session, whatever happens. This means five times a week, and it also means that I finish all my running sessions downhill, so you can run fast even if you are tired and you feel good when you arrive home.

In the winter time, I run up and down hills in my normal runs, nothing specific.

I start specific sessions in April-May, like pushing hard eight to ten times up for 300m on slight uphill sections (not steep, because I am heavy) and run down easy. I like to run uphill to make me sharper before a race. It is really good to develop the leg power that we need in triathlon more than speed, I guess. We do not run that fast in triathlon, except in the last two kilometres of the worlds in Montreal 1999.

Since I am a heavy guy and I have a tendency to build muscles, I try to avoid hill sessions in biking. Also because there is too much suffering. I hate going up and down hills in a specific session. I prefer to go for a hilly ride like a 100km loop including hills.

I have a loop at home: it is a small road with a really long, slight uphill section, and then a very steep climb and a sharp downhill and then a climb again, so you never rest. It is 50km long, and I do it only once.

I have a problem with laps in training in general, bike and run. I can hardly do track running for example. I simply do not like it. On the other hand, I like it during racing. During training, Jurgen Zack (medallist five times in the European championships before having a great career at long distance, notably Roth and Hawaii, Author's note) does 10x2km... I hate that, it is crazy!

Luc Van Lierde

I include hills in my cycling training, but I know I cannot do many because I put on weight.

If I prepare for a course like Nice, I train on long, gentle slopes. If I had to prepare for Embrun I would ride on the Flanders plain because they have some very steep hills. But whatever the hill, I ascend easy.

I never do any specific hill session for running simply because I don't see the point. That said, I think descent sessions must be useful for technique.

Philippe Martin

I set hills in both cycling and running.

In cycling, we do four to five ascents of 3km (gradient ten to 15 percent) with the aim of using the highest gear possible for getting up. This session is programmed for the period of preparation at Easter in Spain. We do not differentiate between men and women for these sessions except in the amount.

Our athletes are very good on the bike, not because they do this type of session, but because they love cycling. Take note: we do not do hill sessions in the days before competition.

When we were preparing for Vuokatti in 1997 (very hilly cycling circuit) the programme was up to the individual and the athletes chose different sessions.

In running, we do ladder work during the whole winter preparation period, consisting of three long series of up and downhill. We do the same on hills in the forest. These are naturally very difficult sessions (zone 4-5), which have the aim of running fast. This develops strength endurance, but we are also looking for changing muscle contraction times.

The limits to hill training? Injuries.

Simon Lessing

Basically I do hills, sitting in the saddle at 80rpm, to be more powerful. Climbing a hill with the biggest possible gear puts a lot of pressure on your knees and this certainly could cause injuries. You can do that for a certain amount of time, but you have to be careful because when your body is tired that's when you can easily get injured. I just generally believe riding on a hilly terrain is going to make you generally stronger on the bike.

Around where I live there are some very nice biking areas where it is very undulating or hilly. I do hills pretty much all year round. But not before a race because I want to avoid hurting my legs.

In the run, we have quite a few trails. I run on trails literally four to five days per week, and these trails can be either flat or they can be quite hilly. Generally speaking, I do one to two hilly runs a week, and the rest of the time it is on undulating or flat trails. And I have one track session per week.

After doing triathlon, I used to go back to South Africa (where Simon is from; however, he chose a long time ago to represent Great Britain in official competitions, Author's note) to my running club and I found myself a lot stronger than the Africans on the hills. Because of my cycling I managed to power up the hill a lot better than a lot of the Africans could. The Africans are very powerful on the flat, but as soon as they came to a hill they were battling. I definitely think that cycling hills helped my strength on the run.

I do not think cycling entitles you to run less, but it entitles you to concentrate more on the basics.

Eduardo No Sanchez

We like to use hills in our training both in cycling and running. I am sure this sort of work helps anaerobically and with strength.

In cycling, the hills we include in our sessions range from 200 to 800 metres and we ride them at a pace ranging from average to hard, covering a total of three to nine kilometres. These sessions always end with a heart rate session close to the anaerobic threshold (five beats under) lasting for 30 minutes.

In running, a typical session consists of a series of six hills of 100 metres followed by a second series of four (to six) reps over 40 metres, all of this very fast. In the same way, the running hill session ends with threshold work lasting 20 minutes.

Personally speaking, I only see advantages in making my athletes do hills.

As for the descents, I always avoid them in running because the recovery that follows is always very long. In contrast, we do not baulk at descents on the bike. It is very important for technique and for finding more speed.

Susanne Nielsen

I love hill work on the bike, but I find it very difficult to satisfy this need in Denmark which is a desperately flat country. So I take advantage when I'm in training camp, in Lanzarote for example. I like climbing long hills at a given pace, decided by the way your legs feel at that moment. I also like the short hills you have to climb with power on a big gear.

On the other hand, I do very little running on hills. Not that I don't like mountains, but rather because coming down is very bad for the legs. And to this day I have not found the hill that you don't have to go down again at some time or other…

Laurent Chopin

I use hills in cycling and running… it's more difficult with swimming!

Basically, I rely, in cycling and running, on two types of session: those aiming mainly at technique and strength training and those with a psychological aim.

In cycling: technique/strength training: high gear work (40 to 50rpm) continuously or varying strength and speed. Physiological development: development of maximum aerobic strength or work at a given pace according to the type of course aimed at in competition.

In running: technique/strength training: every running hill session has a strength training dimension; I suggest sessions alternating volume/frequency. Physiological development: typical session 30/30 or 35/25, the climb at maximum aerobic speed and the descent for recovery.

Apart from the opportunity which hills offer, technically, for strength training and for physiological development, they also let the athlete reach high heart rates at race pace lower than those rates achieved on the track or generally on the flat. This limits the risks of setbacks... so long as you are careful descending.

The difficulties connected to hill work are: finding the hills suitable for the type of work desired; managing recovery; sensibly programming the sessions.

CHAPTER ELEVEN

ALTITUDE TRAINING

Altitude training is a balance between the psychological disadvantages and the physiological benefits.
Simon Lessing

An observation: there is hardly a national squad that does not spend time at altitude, at some time of the season, whatever the sport. Since the 1968 Mexico City Olympic Games (Colette Besson, surprise winner of the 400 metres on the track, had spent, to general indifference, four months at Font Romeu to prepare for the altitude, sleeping in a tent because she could not count at that time on a grant from her federation), facilities have multiplied throughout the world, offering a choice of altitudes, sports facilities and a range of services.

Font Romeu in France, Saint-Moritz in Switzerland, Sierra Nevada in Spain, Arizona, New Mexico or Colorado in the United States, have based, among other things, a not inconsiderable part of their economy on the benefits of altitude to the elite sportsman and his red blood cells.

The benefits of altitude are real, whether one trains or lives there, ranging from the simple stage of oxygenation to the work cycles aiming at the optimisation of aerobic performance. It is still necessary to go to altitude, where the environment lends itself to training adapted to your sport (triathletes are not so lucky, complaining that they cannot find flat courses for cycling or running), for those who possess the necessary knowledge without which they risk damaging their athletes. Although today altitude houses and chambers proliferate, allowing you to live at 4000m altitude without leaving your beloved Parisian suburb or the wonderful Sydney beaches.

Many among the elite triathletes and coaches interviewed have "tried the beast" at altitude and give you in these pages their enlightened, enthusiastic or more measured comments. Others have not yet crossed that Rubicon and explain why.

So take a little altitude… and a long look at this form of training that is a bit special…

Brett Sutton

The problem of altitude is very complex. I observed many contradictory phenomena the more I went to Alpe d'Huez with my athletes. I discovered that some people adapted, some people didn't adapt at all. I've seen some people after five weeks showing no difference, and then after six weeks they took off. Others only needed three weeks and off they went. Or an athlete who left for altitude tired or in poor shape immediately overtrained.

That is why I never take my athletes to altitude if they are not in shape. It is important. And it is the exact opposite of what the Europeans do who use altitude to get into specific shape. The approach is certainly valid, but it is too painful for the body.

In contrast, when they are in form, altitude – if the athletes are used to it – lets you shorten the preparatory training phase. From my days at Alpe d'Huez, I know you don't need 20 weeks of preparation when you are in shape. If you are only given one or two weeks break and you go to train at altitude the base work can be done in only six weeks. In any case not more than nine weeks. Then you need four weeks of complementary work, sharpening, competition and rest. And one or two weeks later, we start altitude work again.

I do not think that it is good to work intensively at altitude for longer than 12 weeks. Yet another rule from my practical, concrete experience on the ground...

It is important to be careful at what altitude the camps take place. Sometimes athletes go too high. I live at 1000m so I think I have some practical experience, and I take my athletes up to 1700m in Australia. We train there, but we don't stay there, so it is opposite to "live high – train low".

I've done medium altitude and trained high some times. And we find we have no altitude secrets apart from some basic rules, like the fact that each athlete reacts differently to altitude.

Once the athletes start to get overtrained or tired, maybe because there is less oxygen in the air, down I go. And I stay down, I give them a rest and then build them up again. At sea level, they can have three or four days off and they recover.

At altitude they don't recover. Sylvain Dafflon is a perfect example: when I had him and he was doing his best, I would give him two to three weeks at altitude and then send him down to Mâcon for ten days before he'd race. Because he was a big guy, he needed a longer recovery. Unfounded rumours started to circulate about him... The fact was I worked out the best altitude for him, and after three weeks it was counter-productive.

If you are at altitude, you must either go straight down and race within 72 hours, or you must go away for between 14 and 21 days. I know it is a bit wishy-washy, but that's what I found.

When they are at 1000m I found that the athletes adapt better. When they go too high you cannot achieve the same tempo in their training.

I think it is a mistake to take distance swimmers at altitude. On the other hand, it is a good idea for sprinters. And triathlon is similar to swimming: the higher you go, the slower the work. And if you do lots of long work it is very tiring.

I am not a proponent of the 'sleep high train low' concept. When our athletes sleep we are trying to have them recover. To put a strain on them by sleeping high they don't get a proper recovery. I have seen a couple of studies that we have done in Australia with

3000m chambers. As much as some athletes were well, a lot of athletes were terrible. Because I think altitude upset their sleep patterns. They did not seem to be getting very much rest at all.

1600-1700m is as high as I go. I found that at this altitude they get a little bit of adaptation and still keep the intensity fairly high. The whole difficulty of training at altitude resides, in fact, in this contradiction: the higher you go altitude-wise the less intensity you can use.

When I was training swimmers, for instance, I used to go as high as I could with sprinters (efforts of 1min or less). I did not have any problem with them. But I found distance swimmers needed to be lower. It is better for maintaining the tempo of their work-out.

Grégoire Millet

I've had ten stays at altitude (mostly Font Romeu) with my athletes in four years, split between January (12 days) and before any declared aim (three weeks each time).

The best plan is to have three stays at altitude a year, with periods of recharging and a final preparation. Our initial plan with a view to Sydney was to prepare the women for the Olympics using hypoxic houses in Vuokatti (Finland) and at Prémanon (Jura), for the purposes of study, including a very exact haematological follow-up (2-3 DPG, EPO, haematocrit, haemoglobin).

This option is a very good alternative to altitude whose limits are today very well known: you don't have as far to go, enzyme and neuromuscular balance is not disturbed, there is a strong loss of muscle power in cycling because the training conditions lead the athletes to use low gears.

However, altitude, including geographical altitude, gives results. All you have to do is look at the aggregate performances of the French women's triathlon squad since 1994, which is when they started going to altitude, to be persuaded.

Isabelle and Béatrice Mouthon

(Isabelle) Physiologically, the interest lies in the increase in haemoglobin and haematocrit in the blood. On the other hand, technically it's a handicap to work at altitude, because the pace is slower. This is where the current practice comes from of sleeping at altitude and training at sea-level.

(Béatrice) Altitude also increases the body's natural ability to control lactic acid, so that blood lactate levels are maintained, so you can return again and again. We have been to altitude some dozen times for three weeks at Font Romeu, and we have noticed the limiting effects of altitude, among them being the inability to work at our maximum pace.

In fact, in a race you never experience the feeling you get at altitude. For example, every one of our rides at altitude ends with a hill, implying a cadence that you never find in a race.

That's where our interest comes from in 'sleep high train low', even though in France the concept is still not well known and understood.

(Isabelle) The length of the stays should be three weeks, but that is not always possible. It would be good to programme a training camp lasting three weeks in winter (once more in January), and two more in the summer (for example, in June and September), depending on our aims (in fact, we go to altitude six weeks before a major goal, and come back down three weeks before) because the more you go to altitude the faster you feel the benefits. In the long term, with the accumulation of experience, it is even possible that two-week stays might be possible. In any case, you feel good for several weeks (three or four) after a stay at altitude, and for an even longer period than the stay.

Karen Smyers

I have not experimented with altitude yet. I have had iron deficiencies in the past, and I would fear such a risk with training in altitude.

It also seems to me that you cannot train as fast as at sea level and that recovery is a real problem. Therefore, since I wish to train as fast as I possibly can and recover well, I do not feel like doing altitude training.

However if I had to race in altitude I would definitely do a specific preparation in altitude.

Lothar Leder

I did altitude training once in Saint Moritz (altitude 1800m) in 1991, and I had a good race afterwards.

I went on my own for three weeks, doing normal base training. I came down and raced well the next day.

I do not do it anymore because the camps organised by the German Federation are held in Font Romeu and I heard bad things about the rooms. But I would return to Saint Moritz, where I also spent years in swimming training camps in April.

Luc Van Lierde

I've been to altitude many times, it is always particularly difficult for a triathlete because you have to find a site with a plateau.

That was why when I went to Sierra Nevada (Spain) it was not ideal for me because there was not a single opportunity to ride on the flat. So I had to get off the Sierra every day which involved a heavy loss of time for each session, two hours of recovery that I could have had in the afternoon.

Altitude camps are useful for two reasons: 1, when you are training for a specific course and you want to peak; 2. because at altitude you do less mileage for the same result, or more kilometres for a better result.

In this respect, I think that the best period for going to altitude is the winter. It is important to remember that an altitude camp takes a minimum of six weeks from your preparation: three weeks there and three weeks 'digesting' it.

At altitude the first five days are for adapting, and the last days three are for light work because it is vital not to come back worn-out from the stay or you would be jeopardising your season.

So, because over the short distance you have to compete a lot, altitude camp outside the winter period is more difficult to organise.

St Moritz (Switzerland), Boulder (Colorado) and Flagstaff (Arizona) are, in my opinion, the three best places in the world for altitude training.

Philippe Martin

The Swiss Federation has long believed that altitude training should occupy an important place in our training programme. Today, we are persuaded of the opposite. Altitude only plays a very small part in improving performance.

On this, we work with Professor Hoppeler (world famous specialist in altitude issues, Author's note).

Among the problems we have identified: hazardous programming; variable effects on the organism; the trails are difficult and boring both in cycling and running; training intensity is different from what you are used to (it is important to avoid over-training).

Now we go for a mixed approach: training at low altitude and a stay at high altitude in January and training in a high altitude chamber later in the season (June or July). This is the direction we are going in now to accumulate experience.

We go to altitude in St Moritz or Davos, the base for the Swiss Olympic Committee.

Simon Lessing

The most important thing in training is to be in an environment that you know. The problem with altitude is that you have to go away, unless you are living at altitude. And going away is just disrupting your rhythm, and I think it is very important to keep your morning, mid-day, and afternoon rhythm of training.

I have trained in Boulder (in the state of Colorado, USA, where many American and foreign triathletes train, Author's note). It was in July. I had been invited to go there, and I needed a change from where I was training. I came down to race at sea level and I felt fantastic. So I am sure it works, but the problem with altitude training is that if you are not used to it, it is very, very tiring. So it is psychologically maybe not so good, because as an athlete you feel terrible, you lose the sensations.

It is a balance between the psychological disadvantages and the physiological benefits.

Eduardo No Sanchez

We've done altitude training since 1997. Initially, we didn't understand how our athletes' bodies responded in the non-competition period. Because the reaction was very favourable, we stayed at altitude close to important competitions.

Nowadays we prepare at an altitude of 1900 metres in Font Romeu and at 2300 to 2400 metres in Sierra Nevada.

Susanne Nielsen

I've never trained at altitude, because I've never had the chance. So I don't know how I would react.

If I were to try it, I would have to be accompanied by someone who was familiar with the conditions that apply and they would have to keep an eye on me. What is more, I would have to go several times to begin to feel the benefit.

These are the reasons preventing my debut at altitude… However, if I did try it I would go in winter because I don't like experimenting with anything in the competitive period.

Laurent Chopin

Even if altitude is not the only reason, you only have to follow the results of certain athletes who are in the habit of living at altitude, like the Kenyans or Moroccans, to dispel all the doubts about what they get from this practice.

So it seems to me that this type of stress situation is good for sportsmen, even if opinion is nowadays divided, notably in scientific literature, because researchers often get contradictory results.

For me, for a stay at altitude to be beneficial, it has to last a minimum of three weeks, with the chance of sleeping at altitude and training at sea-level.

In fact, it is the time duration of the exposure at altitude which is of interest more than the type of effort expended.

If you have sessions at altitude, it will be necessary to spend more or less a long time adapting. And at first you will have to reassess training speeds. It is for this reason that I advocate training at sea-level, at the usual pace, and spending the rest of the time at altitude.

CHAPTER TWELVE

TRAINING CAMPS

Training camps are like dissociated regimen: you have to do it from time to time, but not too often because then you lose the advantage of the uniqueness of the moment, of the specific prepatation. Béatrice Mouthon

(This short chapter is a complement to the Altitude chapter which alludes to the same problems of gatherings outside normal training groups, Author's note)

Training camps are a different time in an athlete's season, a few days or weeks in a foreign environment, a territory to be conquered, for one of the most noble of causes: to learn more, better, differently; refine your preparation; to benefit physically and mentally with a view to the improved results which are to come...

It is also the time of coming together, an irreplaceable social event in the life of a group, whether it be a local club or a national squad. Memories of training in the pine forest, laughter round the table, general sighs at the start of the third session of the second day of the second week...

Yes, but... everything still has to gel, everyone has to have the will to immerse themselves in this world in transit, the facilities have to be right, the food suitable, the sleep sound, and that nothing comes to spoil what should be a puff of pure air...

Hold that image: athletes and coaches have the word. They do not take advantage, but what they say is written in the air of the moment...

Brett Sutton

Training camps should respond to the needs of the athletes. For example, the girls felt the need to do some technical work before the Hungarian stage of the world cup. We responded by organising a week's training camp.

In fact, you could interpret the organisation of training camps as responding to the need for contact between athletes and their coach. These camps at the same time let the coach take control of training by means of physiological and technical data.

Isabelle and Béatrice Mouthon

(Béatrice has been to training camps in the four corners of the globe: in Australia, California, South Africa, Lanzarote and Font Romeu, Author's note)

(Béatrice) The point of training camps is to mentally prepare the athlete, to the extent that any stage is organised at a strategic time of the season with regard to a targeted goal. In this sense, apart from the altitude phenomenon connected to our camps at Font

Romeu, the simple evocation of 'training camp' refers to a privileged moment of preparation and is therefore mentally beneficial.

We are in the habit of keeping a packed suitcase about the house so that the structure-camp does not catch us unawares; quite the opposite, we take pleasure in the camp because we can concentrate 100 percent on our training, because at home our immediate environment (telephone, family, friends, etc.) has a tendency to disturb our preparation.

(Isabelle) Training camp is very important. It is synonymous with competition, close contact with other athletes and with the coach. The camp generates a context which promotes optimal training.

On the other hand, when the camp lasts a long time, living together can generate tension and animosity. A long camp can be useful in that people get to know each other, but can also harm friendly relations between athletes.

(Béatrice) Training camps are like dissociated regimen: you have to do it from time to time, but not too often because then you lose the advantage of the uniqueness of the moment, of the specific prepatation.

Lothar Leder

I do not like being in training camps any more. I feel as though I am in a prison. For example, at Club La Santa in Lanzarote, two weeks is the limit. But I have to do it in the winter time because there the weather conditions are good, not like in Germany. But I prefer being home with my family.

That said, the training with, for example, Thomas Hellriegel is good, it helps you. I like that type of competition. I don't like to live out of the suitcase ; we already have to travel a lot for races, and then the training camps...

Another problem is that I lose my training rhythm when I go to training camps, and when I go to a new destination, it takes one week to adapt, and then I go home...

I find my rhythm with training, food and sleep quicker and better at home.

Simon Lessing

I went to Lanzarote in April for two to three weeks. The main reason why I like training camps is that you become tired of the same roads, the same trails, the same pool every day. It is definitely refreshing, it is good for the head to change your environment. But I don't like the hassle of having to worry about where I am going to train.

So for me the best place to train during the year is at home, because I have everything there, I know where to go, there is no stress, I can relax. So again it is a question of balance.

Laurent Chopin

My internationals do the same training camps as the French national squad. At club level, we organise a camp at the beginning of spring and two camps in summer, each of one week.

I try to vary the places we go to and find spots adapted to the type of training I want the athletes to do.

The programme of summer camps depends on the calendar and is organised around specific goals: these can be camps aiming at undertaking a lot of base work or for cutting the season in two and redoing base work. On the other hand, they can be seen as targeting a competition and so concentrate on sharpening, and tactical and psychological work in groups.

My dream would be to have all the athletes I train under my control. Like a magnet. The system that Brett Sutton has put in place would suit me as well, apart from the fact that I do not wish to take my athletes away from their bases or cut them off from their families.

CHAPTER THIRTEEN

MENTAL PREPARATION

"Let your body speak. You are an eel in the water, they are the rocks. Don't play to their qualities, be the lightning flash, be the lightning that strikes in a unique place."
Christophe Dominici (quoting his physiotherapist
before the semi-final of the rugby world cup against New Zealand.

In elite sport nowadays, everyone agrees that training makes less and less of a difference between athletes, and that other parameters, such as the quality of recovery or mental preparation, are more and more decisive.

Mental preparation is a heterogenous collection of practices and techniques, more or less formalised, of underlying theories more or less plausible: visualisation, neuro-linguistic programming, mental imaging, relaxation, hypnosis…

As the focus for colossal stakes and a mass of ideas and approaches of the most diverse kind, mental preparation does not yet possess the firm rules and incontrovertible knowledge to enable each person to know in which direction they have to go to become indestructible in their heads… which, let us agree, would be better.

What do we do while we are waiting for that moment? Should our elite athletes get depressed for all that? So what? When champions don't have the tools, they invent them.

Brett Sutton

I pay much more attention to mental than physiological aspects in training. It is, in fact, crucial to understand how the athletes you train behave. You cannot train against the nature and psychology of your athletes. You must understand how they function and work and try to extract what is good in them to succeed. If I had trained Emma Carney in the same way as Jackie Gallagher, or Greg Welch in the same way as Greg Bennett, Jan Rehula or Andrew Johns, psychologically the result would have been disastrous.

Good athletes always have good mental preparation resources. Jackie has set qualities which haven't been taught to her by a coach. She has that mentality: what she is trying to achieve, and the goals. Nothing matters, all life is just blown in the wind. You know Simon (Lessing): he is an obsessive, that's all he lives for. But there it's the same. It is very hard to teach that to somebody.

The older guys are used to working for everything and having to earn everything. Now we have our more precocious juniors getting everything paid for them, so they are missing a very valid training area, where they would have to think for their supper... They are never going to make it because they are too soft. Once again, I get into trouble with the federation because I am trying to make them harder and it is not acceptable…

Without naming names, some of my juniors could not conceive of racing Emma (Carney) because they are going to get torn to pieces. That one is a racing animal, she thinks "I am going to kill them", while the other one says: "I did the training, maybe I can do good tomorrow"! That is the problem of mental preparation. My trick is: I bring the juniors along with the killers! And if they say: "Oh! she is furious", I would say: "Yes, that's right, but she has the right attitude and will get the cheque, while you will be asking: OK, when is my next funding?". You can talk to people, you can shout… they won't change until they have decided to learn…

Grégoire Millet

One year I tried the mental approach using mental imagery. About eight athletes took part in the experiment and played the game at the beginning, but it didn't give any results.

Personally, I am not the type of coach who is going to be there during the races. I have a tendency to disappear myself when the races get close. I do not offer my athletes mental preparation techniques. Everything is implicit. I ask them, for example, to work out scenarios which let them envisage different situations. In this way they can anticipate harmful situations.

Isabelle and Béatrice Mouthon

(Isabelle) Mentality is like physiology: some people are mentally strong, others are weak. Béatrice and I are naturally capable of putting up with a lot, we are mentally strong. We are able to surpass ourselves when we have to. Some people are able to surpass themselves in training but come up against a barrier in competition. So they have to develop these areas of weakness. So we don't work on this quality, but we do concentrate on imagining our races, our stress management, our breathing, etc. I have the feeling that France is a little behind in this area, at any rate we are not particularly helped in this department. It's a pity because I would like to take a course.

(Béatrice) In fact, we don't have a problem motivating ourselves for a race. On the other hand, there is a lot of work to do in the area of assimilating technical control. I remember having passed technique correcting tests in swimming, in the presence of an expert in sophrology, and these tests gave good results. Unfortunately, for financial reasons, we have not followed up this experience. I know that this type of follow-up is common in Canada, for example. I am convinced that training loads could be considerably reduced by working on the mental side in the approach to training technique in activities like swimming and running. It is a door that we have half opened here. It is something which is really worth working on, because the part that mentality plays in training has been under-valued.

(Isabelle) Mental approach is all about context. I try to be positive about everything close to a race, to persuade myself that I am in shape, that I am the best and the strongest, and that everything I've done in training was useful and will pay off, so I won't have a reason to reproach myself on D-day. So I have to be positive about the whole approach and visualise the race, the course, the transitions, the opposition, the technical problems that you can have so as not to panic, not to get stressed, to be ready to confront the challenge without questioning the result.

(Béatrice) You have to know how to anticipate all the problems and to be prepared to remedy them so that you don't get upset by a puncture or a lost bottle. Also, when we do a really hard session, we motivate ourselves by thinking: "If I get through this session, I will cross the line first."

Karen Smyers

I have never taken any course. I am trying to reach a positive frame of mind. I can picture myself in races, visualise how I want to feel during a race, achieve confidence and peace of mind in the way training has gone the way I wanted to.

The night before, I do go through the race in my mind, from getting up in the morning and getting ready for the race to how I want to feel during the swim, to envisioning my transitions going fluently, different parts of the bike course that I know will be critical, how I want to feel on a certain hill etc. But I usually fall asleep before I even get to the run! I guess that's a good sign!

Lothar Leder

I never had anyone to teach me how to do it!

But I have my way to prepare mentally: focus. I become egotistic, not nice. If something goes wrong with my training in the last three weeks before an important race (raining, or a bad run), I get really stressed out.

In the last years (before I became a father) Nicole had to move out of our apartment in the last weeks before Roth and Hawaii and go to her parents. Fortunately, I am now getting better! I try to stay cool, to take energy from the training, to not worry about other people.

Luc Van Lierde

I don't work with anyone to prepare mentally. I think that above all the approach should be personal. I have had some problems in the course of my early years which I resolved after my initial races.

Before a big race, and above all over the long distances, I read the list of competitors in order to visualise the way the race will be run, depending on the qualities of the other favourites, their strong points and their recent results.

Philippe Martin

Mental preparation is enormously important for us all. It covers a very big area from visualisation to sophrology, or hypnosis depending on the level of arousal or excitement of the athlete.

In Muskoka (Triathlon world championships 1992), every morning we did mental preparation, relaxation to music, and we forced ourselves to think positive: by visualising ourselves as birds of prey (light on our feet on the course), wolves (stamina) and lions (strong).

Simon Lessing

I just feel that I have to stay relaxed. I used to get very nervous and very afraid. But after being in the sport for so many years, this feeling has gone. When you race competitors throughout the year, you know exactly where you stand.

The most difficult part of the year to race is at the beginning, when people progress during the winter and you do not really know yet where you stand; that's what is the most frightening.

Eduardo No Sanchez

Some of my triathletes have a personal psychologist, others don't. In 1995, we tried something that was not conclusive. Now my recipe for mental preparation is: group work, built on confidence, understanding and motivation.

Susanne Nielsen

My mental preparation is above all focusing on a race, on my strong points, on all the positive things accomplished in the past.

Laurent Chopin

It is clear that mental preparation is largely ignored in training whereas in reality it constitutes a fundamental element in success in competition.

Above I talked about the need of a team behind the athlete (see Chapter Nine- Food, Nutrition and dietetics). A psychologist is obviously part of that.

I launched an initiative of this type some time ago with some of my athletes. I work nowadays at Beauvais with a specialist who places great emphasis on aspects of mental preparation which interest me: sophrology, relaxation, visualisation, etc. Some triathletes in the club are involved in this approach. This specialist accompanies us to the French championships and all the big races in the calendar. He has the advantage of also being a physiotherapist and osteopath.

For this type of preparation to work, the athlete has to get involved. Here, the coach can only advise. It is also necessary for athlete and specialist to be on the same wavelength. Without a relationship of trust, there is no result.

In France, precisely on this subject, we have a big problem of approach because we find it very difficult to trust something we cannot touch and which is not easily quantifiable.

For me, it is inconceivable that a key coach should not be surrounded by an efficient team, including a doctor, physiotherapist, physical coach and psychologist.

CHAPTER FOURTEEN

EQUIPMENT

"I was very naive about equipment, I did not realise how much of an impact it had. I was a 'reverse snob' and felt like I was not good enough to deserve good equipment." Karen Smyers

"It's the shoes that kill the athlete, not the mileage covered." Brett Sutton

There is no sector more sensitive to fashion in triathlon than that of equipment. Every new concept, the whole gamut of original colours, every devastating design attracts the consumer with three heads like grease paper attracts a fly. It has to be said that between the triathlete and his equipment there is a real love story going on.

And for a reason: triathlon is a sporting activity in which equipment occupies an important place. In fact, whether in swimming, cycling or running, the competitor is under the obligation to rely on gear, the choice of which is sometimes very difficult for the unsuspecting consumer.

This is a detailed review of this economic jungle presented by those who try the equipment out the most and recommend without any room for doubt the best.

Brett Sutton

Swimming equipment ? Well... I think you certainly need to have swimmers beforehand...We should surely pay more attention to equipment, but priorities go elsewhere: the way the swims are now it is 50 people smashing and crushing each other...

I think that wetsuits should not be allowed the way they are, they should be one millimetre thick only. That should be the first thing to change in the sport.

I use pull-buoys, small paddles for technique and bigger paddles for strength. I seldom use buckets... You know, pool swimming is tiring, and using buckets will be detrimental to your performance, and further on you have to concentrate not only on the swim but also on the bike and run.

On the bike, I used to have my people more forward in the time trial position. Now the ITU has basically shifted the bikes to a cycling position.

Once again we are giving our sport away to another sport, which is a very bad thing. We pioneered half of the cycling in the past decade. And now we are giving all the technology that our sport has developed away.

I do not believe in having two different types of shoes. The most important mistake people make is to change their footwear. The most important thing is their shoes, and hitting the ground the same way every time. It may sound funny, but in the horse-racing world, the most important thing is the shoe. The angle of the shoe is everything. You put the shoe on wrong? You lose £300,000 with this animal. And what do we do? We put on shoes that are one inch on the bottom or 3cm, and on race day we put on shoes that are very thin. And then you have athletes running around with injuries, and the official reason is too much training... It's the shoes that kill the athlete, not the mileage covered.

I got a lot of people coming to me with running problems, and I found that an interesting idea is to find the right pair of shoes and get used to it. So we are working on this, and it is amazing: 70 percent of the injuries disappear. Not good for Nike, but it is a fact. So the idea is: to train and compete with the same pair of shoes.

Grégoire Millet

I tend to limit the use of pull-buoy for technical reasons. Leg-arm co-ordination, in fact, seems to me to be a key element that should be considered in researching how effective the crawl is. The use of a pull-buoy runs counter to the research into an adequate use of strength and the reduction in resistance which characterises a well-coordinated swimmer.

Paddles are very important but the models have to be varied in shape and form... I often ask athletes to change their paddles over in between series of the same session.

I also like to ask the swimmers to pull a sponge two or three metres behind them so as to slow them down (but not too much) and without spoiling their technique.

We hardly do any sessions in the pool wearing a wetsuit (on the basis that it bores me incredibly). On the other hand we use neoprene in the sea on several occasions at the beginning of the season. There has been a lot of talk about buoyancy as the essential quality in a wetsuit. It seems to me it would be better to talk of glide as well as the suppleness of the material for the passage of the arms through water.

As for bikes, I advise aluminium or titanium frames because they seem to me to constitute the best compromise at the present time without any change in position. Nowadays, we have in fact returned to more classic positions.

On the other hand, for the handlebars, there are a number of biomechanical parameters concerning air flow which have to be respected. So we work with a classic bike allowing us to maintain the forearm horizontal.

Some years ago I used a fixed gear in training. I have dropped that, although I have nothing against it.

The Black Box, and more generally the counters which measure pedal frequency (the Polar X-Trainer, for example), seem really interesting.

Here is a little trick given to me by Sophie (Delemer) concerning cycling shoes: pare down the heel and the sole to gain in weight.

Another trick (now well known in the triathlon world) concerning the swimming-cycling transition: Fix your shoes (already clipped onto the pedals) horizontally alongside the cog with the help of elastic to make it easier to get on the bike and not lose the shoes accidentally.

Concerning running shoes I recommend … a good pair of flip flops (laughter). More seriously, the most important thing to consider about running shoes in competition is the weight while in training absorption qualities are preferred. What is more, you have to be careful to alternate shoes in training.

In competition on the other hand, you can always use the same shoes, by following two pieces of advice to avoid problems: 1) do not use a new pair of shoes for the first time in competition; 2) change your shoes before they are too old.

A trick (for long distance triathlons) passed on by Chilean Cristian Bustos: punch holes in your shoes so that water running onto your feet at drink and sponge stations does not give you blisters.

Isabelle and Béatrice Mouthon

(Isabelle) We now have one piece swim-suits made of more and more hydrophobic material which let us glide through the water really well.

With wetsuits, there has been an extraordinary revolution in their design and in the quality of neoprene. Recently I swam with the latest Aquaman model and I was staggered to find that I did not feel anything, no difference in the arms compared to swimming in a simple swim-suit, while at the same time benefiting from flotation advantages (without being too great). There is hardly any comparison with the wetsuits we had some years ago even. On the other hand, over and above pure stopwatch performance, we gain in the transition, where we no longer have the worry of getting stuck in our wetsuits! Neoprene has become so supple and elastic that we are sure of getting our feet or hands out without a problem.

(Béatrice) I would also like to talk about goggles, and say to which point it is hard to find a pair which is suitable for the eyes and nose when you spend hours training in the pool. And it is also quite important to see clearly.

We use an elastic in training to improve our horizontality in the water. When we take away the elastic after a specific session in the water we are sure that we are swimming flat in the water. We also use the pull-buoy, but together with the elastic.

We have tried swimming with t-shirts or several swim-suits but have now stopped: deep down we are not swimmers!

On the other hand, we use a sample of different sized paddles which give us different sensations. Depending on the model we feel more pressure on the hands or forearm, for example. More generally, it is important to change paddles regularly, simply to experience extremely varied sensations and pressure.

(Isabelle) With the legalisation of drafting, we have taken a leap backwards in cycling equipment. After experiencing a mad period where almost any accessory was authorised, today we have returned to traditional handlebars with a simple U-shape. In a sense, it is a good thing to have contributed to revolutionising the bike industry and, in our return to tradition to have kept certain innovations, like the sizes or profiles of the wheels and the design of the frames, etc. We have also taken a backward leap in terms of the eccentricity of our bikes: it is not as easy to spot a triathlete today.

(Béatrice) With age, we have become more and more sensitive to back problems and our choice of cycling equipment is made with this is mind.

So, in order to optimise our output, mostly in terms of the rigidity of the frame, we tend to retain a certain comfort… In the past, we have opted for a carbon frame whose performance was outstanding but which was incompatible with a course like Nice where the roads are in bad shape, creating excessively poor running conditions. Nowadays, we have turned to aluminium which resolves the problem.

In the same way, after having tried wheels with spokes and with wide carbon rims, we have opted for helium wheels which go anywhere and are light and comfortable.

So the equipment we use today absorbs shocks better and disperses the vibrations in a different way and we no longer have back problems.

In short triathlons you can allow yourself the luxury of a rigid bike frame but not over the long distances where lightness and comfort are all important so you can follow up with a good run.

(Béatrice and Isabelle) We have, moreover, decided to use 650mm wheels which suit us better. We have the impression of being one with the bike, we like its aesthetic proportions, we feel it is better on the hills and the descents and what is more it takes up less space in the boot of the car!

(Isabelle) Of course, it is important to have the benefit of good equipment but it must be underlined that adjustments are also important. So I have raised the height of my saddle by three millimetres and extended the T by 0.5cm and the combination of the two has allowed me to resolve my back problems.

The helmet is also an important piece of equipment but they are all identical today: light, thin and nice to look at, they allow maximum aeration for the skull. They still need to fasten better and not fall onto your glasses when you are pedalling hard.

We are lucky to use cycling shoes which are the most efficient and cost-effective that exist (and no doubt the most expensive). They should be rigid, have no play between the toe and the pedal, nor in the shoe leather when you press down on the pedals so that the transmission of force can be as effective as possible. It should also be possible to put them on and take them off fast, preferring a Velcro strap to more complex systems and that the Velcro should not run the risk of getting ensnared in the chain.

A trick acquired with experience: when you get on your bike and start to pedal with wet feet and shoes that are too new, you can slip and have an accident. Put non-slip paint on the shoes and that solves the problem.

We have not yet adopted the turbo trainer as much as the Australians who have made a fourth discipline of it. It is practical, above all when the weather's bad or we are travelling, for example in Japan, and we cannot train. It is useful for a spin, you can have short, very effective sessions of one hour or an hour-and-a-half. This is another training procedure that we should adopt like hills and transition sessions.

(Béatrice) It is a good idea to have several pairs of training shoes for running, so that the muscles of the foot are not always subject to the same tensions, a little like paddles in swimming. This refusal to accept stereotyping and routine helps to avoid muscle and tendon trauma.

There has been a certain amount of controversy surrounding padding in running shoes where the advantages can be counterbalanced by a loss of sensation in the arch of the foot. Our training shoes are shock absorbent, but less than before; we always feel the ground. We can certainly allow it because our running mileage has gone down.

Concerning competition shoes, we have found the ideal pair and do not want to change them. They are performance shoes. They are light but they can be used. We have to change them after about ten races maximum to avoid injury, because they lose shock absorption and have a tendency to collapse.

We use four to five pairs of shoes a year: two to three training shoes and two to three competition shoes.

Karen Smyers

Long sleeved wetsuits seem to be the fastest for me, as long as I find one which is very flexible at the shoulders. And I found that Quintana Roo has a very good wetsuit, by far the most comfortable I ever have tried on.

I do not like two-piece swim suits that much, because I do not wish to have water getting in at the waist and I hate it when the suit is so tight that it is constricting.

I was very naive about equipment, I did not realise how much of an impact it had. I was a "reverse snob" and felt like I was not good enough to deserve good equipment.

When I qualified for the worlds in 1989, I was given fast wheels and all of the sudden I was passing on the bike those who were passing me before. I really discovered bike equipment in Avignon.

It absolutely can make a big difference, and the faster you are the more of a difference it makes. But you also need reliable equipment because there is no sense having fast equipment if it is going to break down on you!

I tend not to do too much experimenting with equipment: when I find something that I like, that works for me, that feels good, I try to stick to it rather than trying a new one at each race, hoping it will help me gain a couple of seconds.

I have had a quite traditional bike since 1990 (Trek 74.5°), but I decided to experiment with a steeper seat angle to enter the Ironman, because aerodynamics are more important on long distance races. So Trek designed a bike for me with a more forward position (78°).

I have never even tried smaller wheels, but I have heard that what you gain in aerodynamics is lost in rolling resistances (600 and 650mm wheels have a frontal projection which is inferior to the 700mm ones but need in contrast a faster rotation for a given speed, Author's note), so.... they might make sense for smaller persons, I guess not for a person as tall as me. And it is still very hard to find spare 26-inch tyres in the US, though it is getting better now.

I did try the tear-drop helmet once (1990 or 1991): not the most comfortable helmet in the world, it was kind of heavy and... it looked ridiculous! Trek makes all my helmets and I am very happy with them. If I were going for an all-out time trial where each second mattered, then I would probably sacrifice comfort and airflow quality, but in triathlon I prefer to go by the comfort factor.

I got hold of a pair of duathlon pedals for the Bercy indoors triathlon (they are pedals which can have running shoes fixed to them; they are very useful for the running/cycling transitions in duathlon, Author's note), but they were finally banned (they were shown to be dangerous on slopes and, what is more, they destroyed precious track, Author's note). There are definitely scenarios when I would use them. For a 10km/40km/5km duathlon, I would stick to the clip-on pedals because the distances are long enough to make a difference. But for a shorter race, I would consider them.

For trainers, I am looking for comfort, shock absorption and how it fits to your foot.

For a race, I need a little bit of support, especially in the arch, and I look for shoes as light as I can possibly get. I'll go for a little bit sturdier shoes for an Ironman (where you have to run a full marathon, Author's note) than I will for a 10km.

I have never done a winter triathlon, but I do cross-country skiing on my own. I have Blizzard skis.

Lothar Leder

Goggles are the most important piece of equipment for swimming: double stripe, soft so as not to get hurt if you're punched by other swimmers. And since if I lose my goggles I drop out of the race (whatever the water, salty or fresh), I place the goggles under the swim cap. Once I had to swim in Phuket/Thailand without goggles... what a bad race I had...

Not being a good swimmer, I am looking for buoyancy, above all, in a wetsuit. I use Orca. I swim one third of my mileage with a pull-buoy (I am a lazy guy!). I do not swim with an elastic band around my ankles because I sink.

I am a big bike changer. I switch the saddle, the handlebar. One year, I had ten handlebars, I tried them all before Hawaii... I change bike shop twice per year. I simply like to change. I am looking for lightness and stiffness in a bike, and aerodynamics for the Ironman. Ironman and drafting races are a different sport.

For the Olympic distance I use (at the moment) a classic Bianchi bike, sitting back 6 to 10cm, so I look like a cyclist. For the Ironman right now I have a Softride, I am really low in the front and the shifts are in front of the handle bars. Both bike frames are aluminium, titanium is too heavy.

I have tested a lot of helmets. I would love to ride aero-helmets for Ironman, but they are illegal (they do not have ANSI-SNELL recognition). So I use the same helmet (like the Giro) for short and long races.

I started using a turbo-trainer in Australia, with very tough sessions. Now I use it on my own, for recovery, half an hour spinning with no resistance with a heart-rate of 120-130bpm.

I switch my running equipment a lot. For example, I like to run in a brand new pair of shoes in Hawaii. I have been with Nike for ten years, and I know my size exactly.

My training shoes are completely different. I never train in my racing flats, apart from transition training. The racing shoes are lighter, the training shoes are softer (therefore heavier).

I use eight pairs of shoes every year: five pairs for training, three pairs for racing.

Luc Van Lierde

I swim every day in a long-sleeved wetsuit. The essential qualities of a wetsuit vary according to the race. In short triathlons it needs to come off quickly and in the Japanese world cup races I saw some athletes with revolutionary models which really made the difference in this area.

Today, an Olympic distance race is won as much in the transitions as during the circuits themselves.

I use a pull-buoy and paddles in training. The paddle work corresponds to 25 percent of my total mileage.

These last years, a lot of triathletes have adopted a very forward position on their machines. On the contrary, I have defended the traditional, rear cycling position with variations depending on the type of race I'm taking part in. In Nice, for example, my saddle is put back 8.5cm while over short distances it is only 6cm.

I have opted for an aluminium frame, because of its light weight compared to carbon fibre or titanium and I have 700mm wheels. For short triathlons with drafting I have spoke wheels and completely normal handlebars. For races where drafting is not allowed aerodynamics is important which is why I use a more forward and lower position (so my handlebars are 12cm lower than the saddle as opposed to 8cm for short triathlons).

Philippe Martin

The choices in equipment have a real effect but it is also psychological, above all for the women.

We do tests each winter with wetsuits. I notice that there is still an enormous margin in technical progression of the equipment. I don't use the pull-buoy very much at all, preferring paddles.

With the rules imposed by the ITU immediately after Gernika (1997 duathlon world championships, Author's note) there has been a return to traditional lines. It is most important that the equipment be above all of good quality (we want to avoid bad experiences like what happened to Natascha Badmann who got a flat tyre in Hawaii after 50km!).

The Swiss use very traditional bikes, except for Urs Dellsperger who used a floating saddle (only in training) because he had a bad back.

As for helmets, two factors are essential: safety and aerodynamics. Today there are plenty of crazy designs. You might well ask yourself what they would be good for if there is a crash.

Olivier Hufschmidt (former world and European junior triathlon champion, sadly deceased) did 60 percent of his winter mileage on a home-trainer with rolls, mostly to practise balance.

Concerning pedals, 1997 was very revealing about the tactical tendencies and choices for duathletes. Almost everyone chose traditional pedals in Gernika (hilly circuit). In contrast, a large percentage of Thompson pedals (platform-type, Author's note) flourished in Glogow (European duathlon championships, criterium style circuit). That said, the two Swiss Golay and Frossard (who had finished first and third respectively in Glogow, getting away during the bike section, Author's note) had opted for traditional shoes and pedals.

Karin Moebes, world winter triathlon silver medallist in Malles, had the Norwegian team wax her skis…. Skis in the winter triathlons are more important than bikes in traditional triathlon.

Simon Lessing

I do not like wetsuits. I think wetsuits are relatively unfair, because non-swimmers can always bridge a gap.

If I take the regulations point of view, equipment is becoming less and less important in terms of having aerodynamic wheels or bicycles, given the fact that we are now riding in packs.

I now race with standard light-weight wheels with a good 23mm tyre on it, because for most competitors when you have a flat tyre, the race is finished. So I am looking for stronger and more reliable equipment than the one we used to use. I have a suspension system on my bike, which is quite unique, I think, and I like it. I think it is very good for training. It takes a lot of the pain off the road surface.

The choice of shoes depends on the athlete. For running you need shoes that are comfortable and stable. If you are running on trails you need a shoe that you feel stable in and that has a lot of support.

I like to race in pretty light shoes. Considering you are running on your toes most of the time, every year I change my racing shoes. Of course, your training shoes are more important. I like to change my training shoes every two months.

Eduardo No Sanchez

You should be able to get wetsuits (all very similar nowadays) off without ripping them. As for goggles, it is important they should all be anti-fog.

For women, the weight of the bike is crucial, more than for the men. Since Spanish women are little, the frames are small in size and so can be of aluminium. That is not the case for the men who are bigger and stronger.

Lightness is what we are looking for in running shoes: no triathlete will opt for shoes which do not have this quality. A heavy triathlete might opt for shoes which are 60g heavier, but not more. Comfort is one thing, effectiveness and tiredness are another.

Susanne Nielsen

My bike is the most important part of my equipment for me. I want to try different positions, to feel at home, feel how it reacts, understand what will not work, etc. I have worked out the dimensions myself, without recourse to an expert in biomechanics.

Laurent Chopin

I use classic equipment: in training pull-buoy or pull-kick, paddles, kickboards, elastic and flippers; in competition, wetsuit or Aquablade. We are working together with Aquaman to develop the best product possible. Two tricks concerning the wetsuit: you have to get it off as soon as possible (within the limits of the rules) before the water which has got in between the skin and the neoprene during the swim goes. In this way, the neoprene slides over the skin without difficulty and the transition is faster. And to get the wetsuit off the ankles more easily, it is a good idea to put some Vaseline on the ankles before the start.

A strategical trick from the French Clubs cup (Team Time Trial format, Author's note): the first one out of the water goes as far as possible before taking his wetsuit off to avoid a bottleneck and make the task easier for the others. He sets the standard regarding how people enter the transition area.

The spread of drafting, and the end of a fashion, mean that we have returned to more classic equipment than before in triathlon cycling. Gone are the inverse saddle stems, the vertical tubes angled at 78 degrees, etc. We are returning to normal and more efficient bikes.

Elite athletes often have several bikes and so can choose which equipment to use depending on the race. For the rest, it seems wise to me to choose the most versatile machine which is best adapted to your shape and the use you want to make of it. In this area, the most expensive is not necessarily the best.

For wheels, it is interesting to have a training pair and a pair for competition. Choosing a diameter of 650mm or 700mm depends on the shape of the athlete. A good compromise would be to have a 650mm wheel at the front (bike more manageable, less gyroscopic effect, better aerodynamics) and a 700mm at the back (greater inertia). There is, however, one drawback: you need a double repair pack. A carbon-fibre wheel? Only on a flat surface, if there is not a lot of wind and if the road surface is good.

The famous triathlete's handlebars… has lead in its wings. Though it is indispensable in time-trials, it is almost useless with drafting.

There is nothing revolutionary about cyclists' clothing. It should be practical, functional and comfortable. In sum, the cyclist's classic equipment.

A remark concerning the race number: if you are swimming with a wetsuit you can fix it to the singlet/jersey top; if not, it will be easier to fix it with elastic.

The home-trainer is useful for more than one thing: warming up before competition if the weather is bad; to recover from competition or a hard running session; to do specific technical work; and possibly to do multi-transitions home-trainer/track.

Duathlon pedals are very interesting for bike-to-run (run-to-bike) transitions when drafting is allowed, on a flat course not needing a great deal of power. Rob Barel has used them with success. To be efficient they should have a catch for the heel of the shoe.

Running clothing should follow the same rules as for cycling: it should be practical, functional and comfortable.

For shoes, their choice depends on the situation: training or competition, short or long distance. In training, the shoes should be adapted to the particularities of each athlete; for fast sessions, you should use competition or intermediate shoes. In competition, light and dynamic shoes are preferred for the short distances; for long distances, light shoes, intermediate or training shoes will be chosen, depending on the weight, stride length as well as the length of time spent running.

In any case, use shoes which are already run-in and know the places (stitches…) which are likely to cause injury. To counteract these problems, there are pomades which strengthen the epidermis or lotions with lemon juice or alcohol base. Wearing socks is also a solution.

It is important to maintain your shoes throughout the year and not only at the approach of the season.

CHAPTER FIFTEEN

SWIMMING

Swimming is the discipline where a triathlon is lost – the run is where it is won. Grégoire Millet

Swimming can be thought of only in a fluid environment. Swimming needs the most horizontal position possible. Swimming requires that arms as well as legs take part in a movement aiming, at one and the same time, at staying on the surface, keeping your balance and moving forward.

So this is why, of the three disciplines making up the triathlon, swimming is certainly the most technical and makes the most visceral, intellectual and emotional demands. Standing upright and travelling by foot are conditioned into us but the problem with swimming is that it is not.

Swimming is learned over a long period. To swim quickly and well requires patience and qualities that we do not all possess.

One may know how to swim between the four tiled walls of a swimming pool but lose all reference points at sea: the current, the waves, the mists, the temperature of the water, tiredness, the other competitors, constitute as many parasites calling into question a technique and a mastery not always safe from disagreeable mishaps.

In any case, God be praised, swimming has been imposed on us as an appetiser for all triathlons, and not as a dessert, which would certainly be indigestible.

So, if there is no doubt that swimming constitutes an important part of any triathlon (which is confirmed for us in the most resounding of ways in the pages that follow) it is advisable to ask yourself what qualities are needed and what should be taught as a matter of priority to those who wish to carve out a career in triathlon.

It is also advisable to try and learn more about the principles employed to attain a high level, and the sessions that athletes force upon themselves to succeed in the pool and the open sea.

Mission accomplished: our triathletes and coaches plunge straight in, and educate us about what to do in the water.

Brett Sutton

In drafting triathlons, if you cannot swim at the front you will not be in the race. That's why swimming has become crucial in triathlon. We have pace-lines and people just hop on the back. If you can draft, it is another skill. It saves energy dramatically, which is unfortunate again, but this is how the sport is going...

What I try to do for my people who are not such good swimmers is try to get aerobically fit enough to be able to improve five seconds for each 100 m.

If I have girls who can hold 1min 20sec pace for 100m front-crawl for 30 or 40 reps, they are going to be in the first pack because they are physically fit enough to withstand the first 150m sprint. And with the other girls, instead of having them go faster, I'll try to have them go as fast but for a longer time.

I was interviewed at the beginning of the nineties, and I said: "By the end of the century, there are going to be 50 swimmers in the first pack. We are getting that way now with the men. People said: "You are an imbecile," but I am not. I know swimming. It was still so mediocre, anybody can swim 17:30 for 1500m if you've got five people in front of you. In the past you only had a couple of guys in front, like Yves Cordier. Today, we have Benjamin Sanson, Craig Walton, Laurent Jeanselme, Brad Beven, Ben Bright and a few others who can swim really fast. And ten guys in front means that another ten can sit on them because the front pack is now so large that inertia is going to carry the others through. And the same is now happening on the bike, leading to 50 guys rushing into the transition area for the run. It is looking damn stupid, to say it straight. Once it gets to a joke, people, media and sponsors will switch off, while we are trying to have them switch on!

We want something exciting to happen, meaning: changes in the leader. When Craig Walton moves away in a world cup, will he be run down? It kept everybody excited. You must create the opportunities to have people keep attacking. A great race would be if the Olympic distance were the Nice distance. That would be a super race!

I think I make a mistake sometimes: we do most of our work in a pool. And several of my swimmers who swim well in a pool swim badly in open water. We do not do enough work in a lake or with wetsuits. Some of my swimmers can't swim nearly as good with a wetsuit on. So I have to change my mind in that specific area. Having said that, swimming will never be swimming in triathlon. When there are 50 people all of the same speed, you are not going to get one stroke where you are not going to be touching or hitting another person.

And sometimes the contact between competitors is extremely violent: passing a buoy in Gamagori in 1999, Greg Bennett got a punch on the head which could have killed him if he had not been wearing a wetsuit. He floated for about 30 seconds before setting off in the opposite direction to the race, which made the spectators laugh because they found it funny. Without his wetsuit he would no doubt have sunk.

I have two people in my squad at the moment who are as good swimmers as Craig Walton but they are getting out 35th and 36th in world cup races because they can't stand the punching and the kicking and the biting. They are scared people, frightened of the pack. You need to be of a certain mentality to be able to do a triathlon swim. Craig Walton is not a fast swimmer in a pool. He would not be in the top five. But put him in the surf, which he grew up on, and he goes as a shark, he'll swim with Ben Sanson, while in a pool Ben will beat him by a minute-and-a-half over 1500 m. Easy.

One of the problems I face is the number of bad swimmers I have that I have to make good. To succeed, should I programme one big session one day and nothing the next so that they can recover? That is a real problem I have to resolve. I like to be able to make them swim in the morning and the afternoon, and the day when a solid session is programmed it is in the afternoon and it is the last session of the day.

I do not really have a preferred swim session, but we do once a week a main set of about 3km, with short rests. A typical set would be 30x100m, with maximum 10sec rest.

Some swimmers breathe on one and three according to their stroke, others breathe every other stroke on the same side.

Swimmers can hyperventilate if they are not properly prepared. But when they get out of the water with lactate levels lower than 4mmol/L you have to submit to the evidence: they can't be breathing as badly as all that. Hyperventilation comes at a time when the swimmer passes through an anaerobic phase. So you have to learn to swim aerobically. And to do that, you have to swim regularly. If Simon Lessing swims everyday he gets an enormous advantage from that: even if he does an easy session here and there, he is still in the water.

95 percent of all the triathletes that I have seen swim only enough to get competitive for 100m. If you went to any swim coach and said: "I am going to swim four times a week for an hour, and I want to swim 1500m", they would laugh at you.

When we get out of the water, we get out very comfortably, that's the major thing because you have to ride and run afterwards. We might swim 17min 30sec, the same as the next guy. But if he is not doing the training, he will technically (once again motorskill-wise) and system-wise be in big difficulty.

Benjamin Sanson is a very good swimmer... and that is killing him, because he is not doing enough swimming any more. He is still swimming in front of the pack but it is hurting him so much more than years ago... I am sure his lactate level is much, much higher than before. Then he gets on his bike, and he spends the first 10km not as a bike ride, but as a lactate disperser. I used to do the same with Ben Bright, who used to be a good swimmer. As soon as I backed on more swimming, he started to improve. More swimming means more 'consistent' swimming. I had dropped off intensity out of his swimming, because I felt, 'Well, he does not need it'. I was wrong.

And Hamish Carter (a New Zealander, the most consistent of the decade, won several medals in the world championships and won the 1998 world cup, Author's note) made the same mistake with biking (I used to coach him in 1992 and 1993, and then I had to stop because I was a national coach for Australia). He used to be a great bike rider. Very strong. But because he needed to improve his running he stopped doing as much bike riding and went to track sessions and did the athletics track season. And then in the first two triathlon races, he ran 36min off the bike. So he asked me: "What the hell is going wrong with me?" I responded to him: "Hame, go out and start riding again". Get your fitness back on the bike." He had let his strength become his weakness.

Grégoire Millet

Swimming is the discipline where a triathlon is lost – the run is where it is won

In swimming, you have to think in terms of the minimum performance you are looking for and, from the moment you are sufficiently competitive, in terms of the minimum amount of work needed to maintain that form.

Above all, you have to teach adaptability of technique depending on the changing race conditions, notably:

The ability to change breathing patterns

The ability to vary arm-arm and arm-leg combinations

We know, for example, that expert swimmers are capable of adopting a 'catch-up' technique while they are swimming slowly, which disappears progressively when they have to go fast.

These are abilities that must absolutely be acquired in swimming. Expert swimmers are capable of changing their technique depending on the distance of the swim, from 15m to 1500m. In contrast, I am persuaded that triathletes (with some rare exceptions) are not capable of doing this nowadays.

It is too often forgotten in training, but a lot of work has to be done on drafting techniques in swimming. And before drafting in a group, in order to go faster than one's speed allows, you have to learn how to draft.

One example of a session: one swimmer is beating six, while another is beating two, a third is in the wave, either to the right or the left. The swimmers alternate depending on the series to be done and the instructions received.

Drafting is also of interest for a swimmer who is struggling to finish his series. In this case it is close to a hyper-speed session.

Swimming sessions are decided in relation to speed and the main priorities: either strength training or technical work. It is within this logic that I graft on the four styles, the full properties, and, for example, drafting (technical work is not necessarily educative).

The sessions in open water (the Mediterranean, in Montpellier) are programmed in the pre-competitive period and at the beginning of the competitive period. They include interval sessions, with entry and exit from the water in the form of a swim-run transition mainly. The sessions in the sea help you control or improve the specific technical level of triathletes: general orientation, changes of direction, rounding buoys (roll over), body surfing, etc. In this sense, it seems important to me for triathletes to practise with the body-board, which is crucial in some races.

Isabelle and Béatrice Mouthon

(Isabelle) Over the Olympic distance in the world cup the swim is vital and especially the start. You can be a good swimmer, be unbeatable in the pool, but if you have a bad start or don't know how to position yourself then you will finish a long way from the front of the race. So you need to simulate the start of a race, swim in a wetsuit, etc. You should not think that doing what Emma Carney does, swimming 40km a week, will have you coming out of the water first.

(Béatrice) Swimming has become increasingly important these last few years because you have to be well placed from the beginning of the ride to have a chance of winning. However, if I had to put the disciplines in order, I would put running in front of swimming, because running helps you make up the big gaps compared to swimming. In fact, it's the run that is decisive.

I recall the Gamagori (Japan) triathlon which has produced two completely different scenarios from one year to the next: on this completely flat course, a small group of swimmer-cyclists had organised themselves perfectly and taken three minutes out of the peloton, while the following year no one had gone out and the non-swimmers had no difficulty getting back to the front.

In conclusion, you can't safely say that swimming can lose a triathlon. But it is, all the same, necessary to be a good swimmer to have a chance.

(Béatrice and Isabelle) What needs to be taught first and foremost? The Australians would say: aggression! It is without doubt the reason why they beat us so much. As for us, we would say: technique. A remark: the ITU no longer hands out coloured caps to the favourites and therefore they are no longer a target.

Technique (amplitude of movement, energy expenditure) is basic, so as not to use up all your shots with a view to the other disciplines that come after. What is more, you have to be in the thick of it so you don't lose touch during the swim.

(Isabelle) It is fundamental to practise sprint sessions, even without a warm-up, in order to simulate the mass starts in a triathlon. In addition, you have to learn how to put yourself in the right place. Some years ago, I stood right in the middle on the start line. Now I look for the sides, so that I can swim freely without risk of being blocked in by other swimmers. After, everything is a question of tactics: knowing where to place yourself, how to take the buoy correctly, and find your way out when you are blocked in.

(Béatrice) You have to learn how to swim without reference to the sidelines in the water or the stripe at the bottom of the pool. Too many swimmers get confused by open water. Some Americans often train in 50m pools with four buoys and they go round them!

(Isabelle and Béatrice) In training we do 25m sprints which start in the middle of the pool. Since we are not touching the bottom and we start from speed zero, that puts us in a genuine triathlon start, and it makes us think about what to do next. We also simulate sprint overtaking, every 100m for example, in the course of an 800m series.

We don't really have a favourite session but we really like a 10x200m with 3min intervals at race pace.

We breathe on every third stroke and normally do the speed turn. We do the water polo stroke and the dog paddle for strength training. We train at drafting, above all when we are tired. We no longer bother with the order to start every five seconds in relation to our training partners.

We swim in open water, mostly Wednesdays in the summer, which is when our pool is closed. We don't practise dolphining in shallow water with waves, doubtless because we don't have the beaches they have in Australia or Cancun. It's a pity because it's interesting. The Australians are really a long way ahead of us in this area.

Karen Smyers

In races where drafting is legal, the swim has become much more important than it used to be. The packs on the bike are almost pre-determined by the swim. What is funny is that some of the best bikers are about the same speed as I am in the water, so as far as I get out of the water with them, I know that I shall end in the first pack.

In Cancun, for example (the 1995 world championships, the first in the drafting era, Author's note), having a poor swim helped me win the race, because I came out from the swim with several excellent bikers and we gradually made ground on the lead pack athletes who were making considerable efforts to stay in front for three of the four laps. Now if I had been in the front pack, I think I would have done the same thing and it would have hurt me for the run.

But having the choice I would rather swim fast and choose the people I want to bike with!

We are getting to the point where there are going to be enough super swimmers to make a strong group in the front that you don't want to let get away. If you are an efficient swimmer, you have more energy left for the bike and the run. So even if you are not in a lead position, you might have created favorable conditions for later on in the race.

There is also a psychological benefit from being 'in' the race from the beginning instead of chasing it. You are much more relaxed and don't feel panicky like when you are obliged to make up some time.

You need a combination of speed and endurance work to do a good 1500m. I have found out that pure endurance training with lots of middle distance repeats ranging from 300m to 500m works for me. That would really get me in the best shape. You also have to practise hard sets like 50's or 75's, building lactic acid and then learning to go directly into a long swim where you are recovering, bringing your heart rate down and getting into cruising pace; these type of sets simulates race start conditions and the importance of positioning in the first 100m.

Actually, I do not really train drafting when swimming. You have to get used to swimming in somebody's bubbles instead of always starting your sets five to ten seconds apart in a pool. There is a huge benefit in drafting during the swim, so if you fall off a pace line you need to get prepared for a 50 metre surge to get back into the draft and then try to recover and stay with it. Going for a real hard burst in the swim can sometimes save you 30sec to a minute over the course of the swim.

I swim in open water once a week, before the start of the season (so that it's not a shock to your system) or particularly when heading for Ironman, to get used to a sore back and stiff neck if you always breathe on the same side, or even goggle headache. Not far from where I live there is a lake which is around 800m across. There is a marked-out course which I time myself on, straight without stopping.

I have so much experience now that I do not need training specific techniques, but if I had someone new to coach who only trains in a pool I would definitely do right-hand and left-hand turns around a buoy, especially in out-and-back courses, because there you can lose a ton of time !

Lothar Leder

Swimming is the second most important event in a short triathlon, the least important for long triathlons.

It is important to start fast, and have the mental toughness to stay with the pace for the first 400 metres. I never specifically train for it. I did it in Australia, swimming together in a small space. I am not fast at sprinting, if I get punched I do not punch back, and I swim on the outside maybe because I am more scared than the real swim specialists. You will never see me swim on the inside. I panic.

Triathletes have to swim 17min30sec for 1500m to have a chance to be in the first pack. This means swimming far more than what I am presently doing. Unfortunately for me, I do not like swimming, and I have really bad swimming conditions in my hometown. I think you also need a swim coach who understands triathlon.

I swim with my swim and triathlon club mates. A typical session would include: 1000m mixed warm-up; 10x100m and/or 5x200 m. I can only swim 3km in one hour, so I need five sessions a week to cover 20km. My preferred training session is to swim series of 50m together with other people; or to combine swimming and push-ups or stairs. For example, you swim 200m, get out of the pool and do 20 push-ups, and swim 200m again and do stairs up and down. Five series in total. It simulates the transition from swim to bike, with e.g. similar heart rates. I practise swim drafting a bit. We swim behind each other or by the sides. We include this especially at the beginning of the training sessions. We try to overtake each other too.

It is not possible to swim in open water in Germany. Lakes are too cold for most of the year, and too dirty anyway. We train in pools to turn around buoys and to turn without touching the wall. This helped me a lot to get faster at the buoys. In Australia, I even learned to dive at the buoys, to cheat. That's the way it is...

Dolphining (moving up and down like a dolphin, diving to pick up speed so as to pass over or under a wave or go faster in shallow water, Author's note) is also a big issue in Australia, together with the 'in-and-out' (this is training for entering and leaving the water, Author's note). You'd be surprised to see how good Miles Stewart or Chris McCormack (another Australian world champion, this time in 1997) are at this game. Unbelievable! They are twice as fast as the Europeans.

I do specific wetsuit training: stretch cords and then wetsuit sets in a pool. If I had qualified for the Olympics (the German qualification system was not in his favour, Author's note), I would have swum the last two months with a wetsuit in a pool, whatever its water temperature (laughter)! But you can't swim for 5km in a 27°C pool without getting dehydrated.

Luc Van Lierde

The most important thing over short distances is to swim the first 200m to 300m well. After, when you are in the first 12 at the first buoy, it is sufficient to swim in the wake of the other triathletes.

I have been swimming for a long time and the structure of my sessions is always the same: warm-up, pull sets, kick sets, complete sets. I easily swim 6km each session, and my weekly volume reaches 25km. I don't train drafting for triathlon, in the same way as I train alone for running and cycling. I concentrate on long distances. That will have to change if I want to be competitive with regard to the specific conditions that apply over the short triathlon with drafting.

It is good to swim in open water once a week, as long as the weather conditions allow it. With or without wetsuit.

Ten to 15 percent of my swim training is dedicated to technique, but I don't do any specific technical training in open water.

Philippe Martin

Swimming should be a priority for anyone entering triathlon. I make cycling and running of equal importance. The main qualities required to be a good swimmer are balance, technique, flexibility and strength.

Specific training for swimming in triathlon turns on one essential factor: sense of direction. Aas an example, Michael Gross, taking part one day in a triathlon in Germany, was completely confused by the lack of reference points in open water and had swum in a zig-zag.

On a different level, I find that kicking has not been perfected enough. You have to swim rhythmically, but also use the rhythm differently depending on the course. Breathe every six strokes at the start (you have to count on swimming the first 400m in 4min 20sec); then three strokes until just before you get out of the water, where the rapidity of the strokes may increase. That is why I don't use the pull-buoy very much in training.

I have got about 100 sessions programmed on my computer. A typical session? 10x100m above the threshold level, with a one-minute recovery. A volume session should not exceed six to seven kilometres in five or six blocks: warm-up, technique, exercise, technique, recovery.

I don't do drafting in training. One exception to the rule was training for the time-trial in the team European championships. The sessions I programme in open water (in the Geneva or Zurich lakes) aim above all at improving the sense of direction. But you can only do this when the water is warm enough! Even on the Costa Brava we swim in the pool. We don't do any work in open water across the waves (which would have been useful in Cancun).

Simon Lessing

Swimming is one of the most important elements for having a good race. If your swim is bad, you are in the wrong group. It is the foundation of your race and if you do not have a good foundation, you are never going to have success in your race.

I like to do hard intensity work-outs with very little rest, maybe 15x100m leaving every 1min15sec, but it is also very dependent on how you feel. In fact, I also like 10x200m or 5x400m if I feel good.

I never do open water swimming in training. I like to swim in the pool all the time, because you are doing clock-orientated work, intervals in a certain time. The other thing is that open water swim destroys your technique.

Naturally, I have long arms which is a big advantage for open water swimming, which means that generally with my arms I can go over the waves instead of being obstructed by the waves. It is quite funny because I do not swim in open water a lot but I seem to be much better in open water than I am in a pool.

Orientation is something you become accustomed to, after all these years of triathlon. And even before, I was raised in South Africa and did some surf swimming since I was 12 years old, I was much better in open water.

I do not train drafting, dolphining or roll-over (this consists in rolling over during a stroke to avoid a group of swimmers in the way, or to get round a buoy fast, Author's note).

Eduardo No Sanchez

Today swimming has become the most important part of a triathlon, to the extent that it decides the make up of the cycling packs. And sometimes, swimming ten seconds too slow can set you three minutes back on the bike and stop you getting into the top ten of a race at the end.

And being strong in swimming comes back to, above all, being strong technically. That's why we continually revise the content of our sessions so that a swimmer does not do the same thing twice in the course of a year.

My favourite swimming session that I got from an American triathlete is the following: group fartlek, consisting of 6x(50 to 100m), each 50m being slower and slower when each 100m gets faster and faster, the whole being followed by a second block of repetitions of (50 to 150m) using the same principle, until the swimmer can no longer follow the given pace (when the 150m is too fast, so that he gets to the end of the pool when he should already have started the next 50m).

Susanne Nielsen

I should swim more! The problem is that you have to swim so much to improve so little! I have spent so many years improving my cycling, years during which I have not found the extra energy to do the same with swimming. On average I swim 15km (from ten to 20km) a week. I have been to swim training camps – the result? Unfortunately, I did not swim quicker. The effect of the training camps did not last more than one or two weeks, and I ran the risk of getting worse at running. So I decided to save the expense.

I prefer training sessions where the reps are over a longer distance, like for example a 10x200m, which allows me to remain at threshold level and to repeat the same times without having to watch the clock.

Laurent Chopin

Over short distances, the importance of swimming is overwhelming, and even more since the appearance of drafting. Over long distances, on the other hand, it does not represent more than a sixth or an eighth of the total time of the race. That said, we know from experience that in Hawaii it is better to get to the front very early, with everything that that implies.

You can apply the following reasoning: the 1500m swimmer can warm up as he wishes; he is alone in his lane, in a pool with turns and a wall to push off from; he has no problems with orientation; he can control his pace as he wishes: equal splits, negative splits, progressive splits, etc. And above all, at the end of his 1500m he has finished his effort.

A triathlete also has 1500m to swim, but in open water; often cold which poses a warm-up problem; he has to get round buoys, which means changing rhythm and technique; and above all, he shares his piece of water with dozens or hundreds of others who are hoping to get there before him. All of which can lead to collisions, being hit by waves or feet, fighting, etc.

The profile of an Olympic triathlon 1500m is therefore radically different and should be carefully studied, in order to put in place a training strategy that corresponds to this specificity.

Several phases stick out in this analysis: 1) a fast start, faster than the average 1500m speed; fighting, getting free, choice of line: 2) control of this rapid start: loss of speed, which is less than the average 1500m speed; loss of technique; 3) return of sensation and a slight acceleration.

The start session has as its goal the simulation of these three phases and prepares the athlete to respond efficiently to the demands.

An example of the start session: dry land warm up ten to 15min (serious)

6x25m, start every 25sec, swum fast

2x50m, start every 45sec, the first in amplitude, the second in frequency

3x200m, recovery 15sec, with pull-buoy; the first: 100m fast, 100m medium; the second: race pace; the third: 100m medium, 100m fast.

The series should be done twice with complete recovery between series.

Recovery, aerobic and technical work to finish the session

Analysis of the session:

Warm-up: the temperature of the water does not always permit the athlete to warm up sufficiently. It is therefore imperative to get the athlete used to warming up correctly on the beach where the start is situated.

The fast 25m: simulation and learning to start fast.

The 50m: one in amplitude to conserve an efficient technique, one fast for the same reason as the 25m.

The 200m: simulation of race start (100m fast), of loss of speed (100m medium, mental and technical control); 200m at race pace: middle of the race and work at target pace; 100m fast: end of the race and the possibility of accelerating.

Changes-of-rhythm sessions: in long sessions, I try to simulate the start, middle, end of the race, as well as rounding the buoy. The goal is to get the athlete used to the changes of rhythm set out in the analysis at the beginning of this chapter.

An example of a changes-of-rhythm session:

12x150m (recovery 15sec): 4 reps of 50m fast, 100m average; 4 reps at race speed; 4 reps of 100m medium, 50m fast. I do not programme a specific drafting session. One of the reasons being the difficulty of organising it when there are a lot of people in the same stretch of water. But I use it implicitly in the short series when it is possible to swim together.

It is more efficient and comfortable to swim in the wake. That said, when you swim in open water and you have to face problems of orientation and choice of line, being in the wake can just as easily become a problem (contact between athletes).

It is in any case better to be in company than all alone. Unless you are alone in front.

In among the crowd it is more difficult to control technique (turbulence, wash) and you have to be wary of the orientation of the triathlete you are following.

It is always beneficial to swim in open water, though you need a stretch of water at a good temperature..Mission almost impossible in France before the competition period.

To swim in open water gives a feel for the situation, a simulation of race conditions. This is an excellent opportunity within the framework of a start session, both for getting your sensory bearings in a wetsuit and simulating the exit from the water and the transition.

CHAPTER SIXTEEN

CYCLING

Cycling is one of the disciplines where it is easiest to progress, because it is maybe not as technical as swimming, and you are naturally a runner or you are not. Simon Lessing

Triathlon has lived through a true revolution these last few years with the advent of drafting in cycling (the legalisation of sheltering behind others and formation of packs which dates from 1995. Before, the cyclist in a triathlon had to ride alone under threat of disqualification, Author's note) totally changing the tactical, physical and mental approach of our sport.

Before 1995, in fact, triathlon was considered an individual sport in its purest state. And cycling training was largely summed up as preparation for an individual time-trial sandwiched between swimming and running.

Since 1995, athletes have had to relearn how to ride, this time together, in competition as they do in training. New race strategies have been devised, pitting swimmers-cyclists, swimmers-runners, and cyclists-runners against each other. New types of physical and mental preparation have seen the light of day, highlighting the quick reaction duality to the detriment of consistency/stamina. In fact, the athletes have had to bring themselves, and not without regret, to return to more traditional bikes, after contributing to revolutionising the cycling world...

The athletes and coaches who worked together on this book have all lived inside the throes of the drafting revolution. They have all had to completely rewrite their scripts to profit from the new sporting deal. And they have come through it all rather well considering what they have won! How have they done this? That is another story...now find out.

Brett Sutton

(Many of the facts relative to cycling have already been mentioned by Brett in the preceding chapters, Author's note)

On the bike, you can be anybody. Even I could be sitting in the pack. I mean that seriously, and this is why I do not like what is happening in the sport today.

I brought over an athlete (whose name I will not mention) who is a good runner and whose swim has improved remarkably. But he could not ride, so he lost eight minutes on the bike in non-drafting races in Switzerland... and then he went to several world cup races and each time he got off in the first pack. With drafting, triathlon is very disappointing... you don't have to be a triathlete anymore, which is unfortunate.

My athletes do as little riding as possible. I ask them to always use a big gear. Don't misunderstand: I am not trying to turn them into donkeys, quite the opposite. But experience has taught me two things about pedal cadence: first, that a big gear raises heart rate and lactate levels less, which is an enormous plus with regard to the run which comes later; the second, that my athletes should never ride at a faster cadence than their stride frequence. So if an athlete runs at 90 strides per minute he should ride at a lower cadence. This is in order to optimise the bike-to-run transition, by favouring the athlete's comfort. For example, Joanne King rides at a cadence of 76 rotations a minute, Loretta Harrop at 84rpm and Beth Thompson is between the two. These cadences are decided by the body profile of the athletes, notably the length and strength of their lower limbs. So, Loretta who is small, has short limbs but she is very strong in the lower body, the opposite of Joanne who is very big, scraggy. With the men, Greg has a cadence of 70 on the bike, while Andrew has 84rpm. On this subject I would like to point out that the pedal cadences suggested to my athletes have risen these last few years since we hardly ever do individual time-trial. Everything depends in fact on the strategic position that my athletes occupy in the race. So, Greg Bennett often rides at the front of the pack, because he knows that to win a race the pace on the bike has to be very high. That is why he has a very low cadence. With the women, Loretta will always be in front because she is one of the fastest swimmers on the planet and we do not consider in her training that she might ride in the pack. On the other hand, since she is much smaller than the men we think that her relatively high cadence of 84rpm constitutes an acceptable compromise for her, all the more because many of the circuits in the world cup are technical with bend after bend in not very wide streets or with small hills which need climbing out of the saddle.

However, whatever my runners' profiles, they have drafting sessions once a week. It depends on the coming race, if they'll be doing loops, etc. They'd rotate on a 15sec or 30sec basis for example. We don't do motor pacing, simply because we don't have these training facilities.

I don't have much experience about mountain biking apart from the fact that you can break your collarbone quite easily. So I don't like my athletes doing it, once again because of the opportunity for injury. In Australia it is not as big a thing as it is in Europe.

If people want to include mountain-biking in triathlon to make it environmentally more friendly that's OK, but that's not triathlon to me. And winter triathlon should not even be called triathlon. It is not triathlon.

My favourite session? An individual time trial. 30min for the guys, pushing hard. For the girls, it depends: it could be 30min, could be 45min or could be one hour. But it has to be longer for women, definitely. Because they don't have as much testosterone and they recover quicker.

Grégoire Millet

Strategically, I favour the waiting game, "á la Fattori". It is a less noble strategy, but very productive. In training terms it means: do a lot of base work, but with not too much intensity in cycling, and transfer the hourly volume onto strength training and running.

I pay a lot of attention to drafting and more particularly to the quality and effectiveness of taking relays in the lead. That's why my athletes take part in bike races.

I would like to do more track cycling and work with a motor pacer, but we don't have the facilities (there isn't a track in Montpellier). That said, I do not miss an opportunity if it presents itself: in 1991 our preparation for the world championships on the Gold Coast took place in Nouméa and there we programmed a lot of track. More recently, the French women's team had a training camp with the FFC (French Cycling Federation), once again on the track.

Isabelle and Béatrice Mouthon

Drafting has totally changed triathlon. Before, a swimmer-cyclist could aim at winning. Nowadays, he gives way to the runner. We have joined a cycling club in order to get used to the numerous changes of pace generated by the rule changes that today legalise drafting. Before, we were able to go with the pace without a change of rhythm because the race was similar to a time-trial. So training today has more changes of rhythm and practising curves technique than real base or specific work. In fact, we do more maximum aerobic power than threshold work because we have less use for it.

All of which means that our cycling sessions have completely changed: we do short intervals (reps from two to three minutes, more lactic), when before we did many intervals of 20min effort.

Of course, drafting is included in training, the two of us or more if possible. The reason we train in Boulouris is because we train with the men and the conditions approach those of a real race.

For us it is clear that we have to go to the school of cycling: to ride through skittles, pick up a water bottle, ride over a board, learn how to prevent falling, avoid potholes, to feel at ease in the pack, to save our energy instead of being permanently under stress. French triathletes learn more how to do mileage than to concentrate on technique. It's a pity.

(Béatrice) My favourite session is a 45-45 interval, 45 seconds on a high gear coupled with 45 seconds at a very fast pedalling cadence, all done in a period of nine minutes, repeating the whole three times.

(Isabelle) As for me, I love the long sessions with a climb to a mountain peak, for example. It is a convivial trip par excellence, ideal preparation for the world cup races (laughs)!

We do very little mountain biking because we live in a hilly area and we are afraid of getting injured. So we favour cross-country skiing in the winter as a safer variant in our training.

(Béatrice) In the past, we did track sessions, especially when we were preparing for the Bercy indoor triathlon. It did us a lot of good and it was good fun. Again, you need a track near you… It is a bit like a home-trainer, you optimise your time: in the space of an hour or an hour-and-a-half you can do specific work (maximum aerobic power work, hyper-speed) very seriously, by being able to quantify it very precisely, with possibly the help of a Derny (motor-bike pacer). It is easy to use and enjoyable.

(Isabelle) I had the opportunity to work behind a Derny when I was preparing for Zofingen. I remember a ride of two hours during which I crossed hilly terrain for 90km! I only had a little bottle with me, I was so thirsty and my mouth was so dry that I could not even tell the driver of the Derny to give me a drink or slow down.

Karen Smyers

It is the part of a triathlon where you can gain or lose the biggest amount of time. There can be a huge difference in abilities on the bike, although when you get in a drafting race it becomes a bit less important. Once again, cycling is important because the better the condition you are in, the better you will feel for the run.

To be a good cyclist-triathlete you need to practise surges, cover breaks, as well as the start: you need to go all-out in the first two to three minutes on the bike, catch out as many people as possible and prevent as many people from joining your pack.

I go for a group ride once or twice a week with riders who are strong enough that if I lose the draft I get dropped. So it really keeps you on your toes. I might have as much endurance as they do, but because they've got more power they can go harder than me for two to three minutes, so it is really a good way for me to practice. Sometimes, I am going so hard that I am building up lactic acid and I can't really hold that pace for long. So I think if I just stick with them for another minute or so they might be the ones in trouble and I'll stay with the pack!

My favorite workout is probably doing hill repeats. I like the structure of it. I sometimes get bored going out for long bike rides, so it is good doing hills. They provide short sessions but very, very high quality and I like to be comparing my times from week to week and see measurable improvements. I take enough time off in the winter that, generally, the whole year I can see myself getting more and more in shape. So I like once every couple of weeks going back to the same course and watching myself go up the hills faster. I like the challenges, I guess!

I haven't really done any structured motor-pacing until now, though I think it is actually a great tool. In fact, we maintain a much faster pace in my group riding than I would ever be able to do on my own. We often ride 30-miles-an-hour where if on my own I would probably not get up to more than 25 to 26mph, so it is kind of like a motor-pace when I do my group ride. There is probably great benefit in doing structured motor-pacing.

Lothar Leder

Cycling is not as important anymore for short triathlons… You can survive on 200km a week only. Sometimes, I do not even do my long rides anymore if I have another race the following week-end. In contrast, skills have become more and more important over short distances. Personally, I push big gears, I do not spin (around 70rpm).

I have a goal for a week (for example 600km in the winter time or when I'm preparing for a long triathlon) and I go for that. And I try to ride with people, it's a social thing (I don't like to be six hours on my own in the woods). These are my principles.

My preferred session is a 40km recovery ride, along the beach! Or (more likely in Germany) a 160km ride, stop halfway for a coffee and then go home faster.

In Australia, I used to do time trials every week. In Germany I don't do it. Lazy... But if I could find someone to do it with me, I'd do it.

Fifty percent of my mileage is based on drafting when I train for short distance. Of course, when I prepare for an Ironman I cut it down, and most of my bike training has to be done alone, in order to bring the heart rate higher.

I did motor-pacing before the 1999 worlds in Montreal for example, to get really sharp. I do neither motor-pacing in the hills, nor on long distance: I can find no one to ride the motorcycle in October when I prepare for Hawaii. I did it once to prepare for Roth, but it did not help.

A typical motor- pacing session would be: 60km at 80 percent, which means 48kmph maximum average. I start by spinning (although on a big chain), and moving to bigger gears towards the end. The point is not to ride 60kmph (which I could do), but to find a coherent and consistent cruising speed, with respect to what the racing pace will be.

Luc Van Lierde

Over short distances, it is enough to stay in the pack or in the lead group and wait for the run. The situation is different over long distances where cycling is more important than swimming.

The main principle that directs my cycling training is spinning. In my winter cycling training, I make sure my legs are turning at between 90 to 100rpm. Pedal flexibility should be as good for short distances as for the long. I know that a lot of athletes go for 80rpm over long distances. In my opinion a mistake. Elsewhere, if I train over undulating terrain I quickly build muscle (up to three kilos), and that effects me afterwards in the run above all over short distances. So I do a lot of training on the flat.

What is more, I have the habit of never training with my triathlon handlebars in winter not even if I have a competition coming up. If you always train with this handlebar, your back muscles no longer do any work and they lose their strength. When I prepare for Hawaii, I start my handlebar preparation just three weeks before the goal.

From May onwards, I ride once or twice a week in a group. I know it's a mistake: you have to ride with a pack at least twice a week throughout the whole year to prepare for short triathlons in the best way.

I train with a motor pacer before races. It is equally useful for long and short distances. The difference lies in the average speed as well as the time it is sustained. For short triathlons, I look for a speed of xmph for one hour while for the long distances I opt for a slower pace for three or four hours.

Philippe Martin

Taking into account the importance running has in triathlon, cycling training should aim at starting the run in a relative state of freshness. Or you can get away on the bike in order to later control the run! So specific cycling training in triathlon today is… less training mileage with short, intense rides.

The Henniez team (the most successful team in the world, it has included athletes such as Markus Keller, Andrew Johns, Christoph Mauch and Peter Alder, Author's note) specifically trained for drafting for the team European championships, the European championship for Clubs and the France Ironman Tour.

Among the sessions I give my athletes, I particularly like the following quality session which is done in the base period: 4x5min but pushing the pace in the last 30sec of each set, needing a brutal pace change compared to the average pace.

We do a lot of mountain bike work in the course of the winter. It is excellent for developing technical expertise (balance, pedal cadence). In winter at St Moritz, the non-swimmers (for example, the duathlete Daniel Keller) train on mountain bikes in the snow.

There is a covered track in Geneva and an indoor/outdoor track in Zurich which sadly we do not have access to. We do tests on the track: in particular we are studying gears corresponding to the lowest heart rate.

Some Swiss athletes (among them Natascha Badmann) train behind motor pacers. They do short intense rides, two days before a race. It is hyper-speed work.

We use the home-trainer a lot in the winter, because in Switzerland the climate is not good. I have at my disposal ten different specific sessions on my computer.

Simon Lessing

Cycling is one of the disciplines in which it is easiest to progress, because it is maybe not as technical as swimming, and you are either naturally a runner or you are not. There is always quite a large room for improvement with cycling. And as a person who does not come from cycling as a background, I definitely over the years improved my cycling through hard work.

When I train in a group, we rotate. We train at a faster tempo than cyclists do. We go for a two-hour bike ride at 35kmph as opposed to cyclists who will ride for five hours at 30kmph. I think this is really the only difference in my bike triathlon training. I don't think we can make any sort of comparison between triathlon biking and cycling because it is absolutely not the same sport, and the training we are doing is absolutely not the same. In this context we might refer to the career of Jonathan Hall. Jonathan was a cyclist (from the Australian Institute for Cycling) before becoming a duathlete. Jonathan has been concentrating on cycling all his life, he is Australian individual time trial champion, and finished eighth in the ITT in San Sebastian, the year he won the duathlon world title. Is there much room for improvement in triathlon cycling as opposed to swimming or running? I don't think so, I don't think that there is any triathlete who can match pro-cyclists. Not too much can happen in a 40km bike anyway, while a lot can happen in 250km. And the problem is that everybody is trying to save energy for the run.

I do a lot of mountain biking in the winter time. It helps me a lot to get into shape. You are working not only on strength but also on velocity. If you have a very hilly terrain it is a very good thing for you, it also helps your bike technique. The only problem is that you can't do it every day.

I do a lot of intervals on the Vitrolles velodrome in summer. We do a ladder with some friends, and this is great because you can get up to pretty interesting speeds and you are working with other people. You do not have to worry about cars and you really have a sensation of speed. This is what I really enjoy about short distance racing: it is the intensity and the speed.

Eduardo No Sanchez

Cycling has lost its intrinsic worth in triathlon with the legalisation of drafting. Only the difficult courses allow you to play your game well and only so far as you have done the specific training for it… All the Spanish triathletes are in a cycling club and so are inured to the situations current in triathlon.

We use mountain bikes in winter, because the present make-up of the triathlon (with drafting) has made all aspects of this discipline more important: balance, concentration, change of pace, descents, associated fear, etc. Yes, mountain biking helps you to cultivate all the technical baggage which has become more and more necessary in triathlon.

I use the turbo-trainer once or twice a week at certain times of the season, so as to improve strength, raise the anaerobic threshold but also because it is fun and allows you at the same time to do some very solid work.

Susanne Nielsen

Cycling takes up most training time, from 12 to 14 hours a week for me. I ride on average 350km a week, sometimes more when the weather allows it. I prefer the long rides more than anything else. Friday and Saturday I ride in a pack to simulate drafting conditions. In contrast I don't take part in races because I think it's a waste of time riding with women: they don't like going fast and I don't want to waste two hours riding at 25kmph waiting for someone to speed up. I don't do mountain biking because I don't master the technique sufficiently and I'm afraid of falling. It's not worth it.

Laurent Chopin

Over short distances, it is the least important discipline, with some rare exceptions, like the 2000 Perth world championships (it was in the ride that France's Olivier Marceau built his magnificent victory by gaining almost a minute-and-a-half over his main rivals. In contrast, the minute's lead he built up in the Sydney Olympic Games some months later was to prove insufficient, Author's note).

The culture of short distances is more oriented towards swimming for the moment. Cycling is more often a transition between the swim and the run. In the future, I think that cycling will re-establish itself, with athletes capable of opening up gaps, of making attacks; in a word, using all the tactics that make up cycling. That has already been noted and will be worked on.

Over long distances, the problem is completely different. To be a good cyclist is a major asset because of the distance and because drafting is not allowed.

In training, sessions have changed, but it is still important to be a good cyclist and be capable of responding to attacks, to adapt to all the situations that arise, and to start the run fresh. In fact, you benefit from the cross training effort (the work done in cycling benefits the run and vice versa).

Cycling is the least technical of the three disciplines that make up the triathlon (technique is determined by the machine). Under these circumstances priority will be given to physiological work.

Today, drafting and technical courses mean that the athlete has to be comfortable on his machine and not waste time and energy on bends, in attacks, and not to make gear change mistakes.

Cycling follows the swim and comes before the run. In these circumstances, triathlon cycling cannot compare to pure cycling, even though drafting is allowed over the short distance and the athletes attack, open up gaps, change pace… Over long distances a parallel can be envisaged with the individual time-trial, if only because you are more likely to find people on a Long-Distance than an ITT. So the solo effort becomes relative.

I have devised so called mixed sessions, the result of two lines of thought: 1) Why should a cycling or running session have a unique physiological impact while in swimming the same session explores several energy pathways? 2) What type of session can be given to athletes so that they get used to the many changes of rhythm placed on them by drafting?

An example of a mixed session:

Series of 3x10min (recovery of 4min between each set): 3min at race pace; 1min easy; 1min at maximum aerobic power; 2min at race pace; 1min easy; 2min at maximum aerobic power.

The goal of this type of session is to be capable of maintaining an average high level pace, with the possibility of going faster, then recovering without slowing down too much, and to do this several times without a detrimental effect. It is my preferred session, the same as the start session in swimming because they are the most specific and most representative of the triathlon.

The part drafting plays in triathlon training depends on the place and the number of athletes, etc. When I coached at the Racing Club de France I always programmed drafting in all multi-transitions sessions. Today, when we are at training camp, the development sessions are always done as drafting sessions. And when the athlete is at home and trains alone, the response comes of its own accord.

You can, of course, imagine all sorts of things in advance, but it is coming out of the water that decides which strategy to adopt in the end. That said, it is possible to imagine all sorts of different scenarios. With a big team like mine and very different athletes, it is difficult to prioritise one over the other in a sport which is above all very individual. The decisions are taken in common about a number of possible situations, and depending on the form and goals of each athlete. Among the strategies worked out, we of course take into account the profile of the circuit.

When the opportunity is offered, I make my athletes ride behind a motor pacer with an experienced rider. It is useful, but it means having a motor pacer and an experienced rider at your disposal.

I did several sessions at La Cipale (in Vincennes, Author's note) in the past and the experience was very useful. On the track, we worked in productive conditions and at well defined speeds, all of which is very good for technique. In fact, the coach enjoys being able to follow and corroborate everything because his athletes are at all times under his nose and in his hands.

Practised alone and in the form of bike-and-run (see the Transition Chapter, Author's note) mountain biking is an excellent compromise for teaching, in total safety (since you are not on the road), the cycling basics to young people.

CHAPTER SEVENTEEN

... AND RUNNING

Technique, always and above all else: footwork, the pelvic position, the arms, breathing, in order to have the most efficient and economical stride possible. Béatrice Mouthon

What could be simpler and more natural than running as a sporting activity? And what could be harder, when the technique goes, when the legs no longer want to carry you, when your will deserts you?

So, imagine the hell that competitors feel (maybe you) driven into a corner in the course of the final event in a triathlon, after having already swum and ridden like mad, and doubtless used up their last reserves more than is reasonable.

Elite triathletes succeed in running where most of us fail: after a strategically and physically perfect race in swimming and cycling, they approach the run with a freshness, technique and conviction which we are cruelly lacking.

How do they do it? Here in these pages (which obviously repeat the preceding chapters) are their priorities, their approach, and their winning tricks.

Brett Sutton

Speed seems to me fundamental for the run. But once an athlete has developed what I can see as the motor skills pattern to run fast, then we'll go out and start running hills once a week.

All my juniors are practising learning to run. I just keep on with that theory that I teach them the technique first and then we worry about other things. Short stuff, like 100m, 200m. What I find is that if I teach them a good technique they won't get injured when we go out and do longer sessions. If they don't have that technique it does not last three weeks before they break down. When they get tired and go out running on trails they get injured. So I keep them on straight roads or I keep them on a track, and that's why people say: "This guy is a maniac, they run on the track every day". I run them on the track because I know it is flat, I know I can watch them, I know we can work on technique. And once I believe that their technique is in place and won't break down, they may start going into the run pattern programme. And I do the same if the swim is weak. We do many repeats over short distances, working on technique, and when the technique is there, then we can start on a longer programme.

My favourite session is a series of 200m or 400m, at or above race pace. Not longer than 400m. And up to a maximum of 10km for that particular work-out, including warm-up and down. Which means not more than 5km for the main set.

Grégoire Millet

To be world triathlon champion today you have got to run less than 29min for 10,000m for the men and less than 33min for the women.

(Other remarks by Grégoire concerning running have already been mentioned in the preceding chapters)

Isabelle and Béatrice Mouthon

(Béatrice) Technique, always and above all else: footwork, the pelvic position, the arms, breathing, in order to have the most efficient and economical stride possible.

(Isabelle) Running is inborn, but depends very much on training as well. In this sense it is very important to be overseen by an expert who can give you advice, either from trackside or via a video, which is even better because then you can observe your own technique.

I like track sessions. They seem the most important to me and the more likely to help me improve. My favourite session (though I do it less nowadays) is a 2x200m, 2x400m, 2x800m, 2x400m, 2x200m, with a recovery equal to the time it takes to cover the distance. What is more, the time for 400m should be double that of 200m plus two seconds, and the 800m double the time for the 400m plus four seconds. In fact, if I can, I try to do the descending part of the pyramid one second faster.

Karen Smyers

It is probably the most important part of the triathlon now, especially with drafting. And even if you are in the second pack, there are always a lot of people that you can catch if you are running well. People are focusing more and more on the run, so the times are getting faster and faster. You are coming closer to times that you could expect in regular 10k road races.

So the training has to be a little more speed-oriented and you have to be sharper for each race. You can't simply be strong, you have to be fast. The triathlon run is coming more and more down to sprint finishes, so you've got to learn how to have a kick at the end. I personally need to get away earlier in the run. (Karen learned this to her cost in 1993, the year in which she was beaten in the sprint for the world title in Manchester by the Australian Michellie Jones, Author's note). In order to do that, you have to learn how to kind-of surge and break people.

There are a lot more tactics that you have to learn, it is a lot more like a regular road race nowadays where strategy becomes more important than just running as hard as you can for 10km !

I really enjoy track sessions. I tend to like structured workouts the most, and things that are measurable. I like doing a longer interval than a shorter probably because I am better at that! One of my favorite workouts is probably doing 3x1mile, if I am feeling good (if I am feeling bad, I hate that workout!). My best time at this distance is 4min 48sec, but I have done a 4min 24sec 1500m, which is a bit faster than this.

Lothar Leder

Whether short or long, the most important part of a triathlon is running. A lot of decisions are made in the run. You have to maintain your technique, you must remain composed and smooth until the end of the run.

At the moment, I train 80 percent in the woods, and 20 percent on asphalt. For Ironman training, I do my 30km runs on asphalt, exactly measured. I train more in the woods to avoid the traffic and the injuries, and to enjoy it more. I think that off-road triathlon has a great future, but it is too hard for me!

My favourite session is the 8x300m uphill session (See Chapter 10).

I do almost no track session because I have no coach. If I had, I would expect him to watch me, my technique, my times, to be there, to motivate me. My favourite sessions on the track are 10x [200m fast (29sec) – 200m slow (active recovery)], and six to 10x1000m (3min pace, recovery 400 m slow). With a coach, I would probably do 400m and 250m.

Luc Van Lierde

The run is the most important part of a triathlon, whether short or long. Over long distances it is the last 10km that make the difference, while with the short, the transition and the first two kilometres are the most important.

Running training for short distance is more specific and technical. In this, the Australians and some Europeans are the best right now.

Before specialising in Hawaii I did a weekly track session and I added a second six weeks before the important competitions. After Hawaii, I do no more than five track sessions a year which is obviously a mistake when I come to line up for a short distance race. My track sessions are of three types: short intervals (150 to 200m); longer ones of 1000m or 1500m at a set pace, after a series of short reps; and reps of 400, 800, 1000, 1500 where I'm looking for a steady pace.

I love long runs in the country. However, road running is also important to maintain and refine your technique which varies from short to long distances.

Philippe Martin

Our athletes are traditionally less good at swimming, and are better off making it up in the run. Our aim is 30min for the 10,000m.

A typical session? During the competition period I love doing a 6x400m at threshold level or greater (103 percent) with a recovery of two to three minutes.

Simon Lessing

I think that running and swimming are equally... No, I think that running is definitely more important than swimming, because if you are a non-swimmer and if you are lucky you will make up time on the bike, while if you don't have a strong run, this is the end of your race. So I agree with Grégoire Millet that "you lose a triathlon during the swim and you win it during the run".

Once again, whatever the session and whatever the discipline the important thing for me is to enjoy training and to feel good. That said, under those conditions I love running for example 10x500m.

Eduardo No Sanchez

The evolution of the triathlon today means that 20, 30, 40 competitors can get off the bike in the same pack, which makes it vital to have all the assets necessary to make a difference in the run. That said, for all the reasons given above, swimming remains the most important of the three disciplines of a triathlon.

My favourite session is a hill workout (described in Chapter 10)

Susanne Nielsen

I run between 50 to 65km a week, peaking at 75km. I don't do track because my coach thinks that a 5km (or 7.5km) is a better recipe than a track session. I love running one hour or an hour-and-a-half in the woods because the sun is not as hot and the terrain is more varied and wild.

Laurent Chopin

The run is the decisive part of most short triathlons. Its importance, with regard to swimming, depends in fact on the way the race is run. A group of swimmers can stay out in front on the ride and can run to win as they leave the bike park. In contrast, the cyclists may regroup and it is then the run that makes the difference. Over long distances, the run is as important as the ride.

To adapt an Emile Zatopek saying: "It is not only necessary to run fast, but to run fast for a long time". So it is important to develop running technique, a little like in swimming. In the absolute sense, the athlete needs to exploit his full potential in the run, despite the transition.

I have already spent a long time developing the question of the principles of training by concentrating on pace, session types, work on fatigue, transitions and the fact training must be viewed like a triathlete and not only like a runner (see preceding chapters).

My favourite session? A fartlek in the country á la Kenya.

A mixed running session (See cycling mixed session in Chapter 16):

2000m at dynamic threshold pace (recovery: 2min20sec).

3x200m at maximum aerobic speed (recovery 30sec between each 200m, 1min30sec after the third 200m).

1000m at dynamic threshold (recovery 1min 10sec).

3x300m (150m at maximum aerobic speed, 50m relaxed, 100m at maximum aerobic speed, recovery 40sec, then 1min 30sec after the third 300m.)

1000m at dynamic threshold (recovery 1min10sec).

3x200m progressives from one to three, the second being run at maximum aerobic speed the first two seconds slower and the third two seconds faster. The aim here is to maintain a high average rhythm with repeated pace variation without destroying the triathlete race base.

EPILOGUE

Five years have passed between the moment when the idea for this project saw the light of day and the present moment, of its publication in English. Finishing the book was tinged with both relief and sadness.

They were years of doubt, punctuated by the very privileged moments I spent with the willing men and women interviewed for the book. Star athletes, illustrious coaches, bearing with them an encyclopaedic knowledge, the substance of which had to be extracted without betraying the experience and feelings of each and every one.

I had written books on the triathlon before but there was something lacking, to which this book acts as an indispensable complement. With age and experience I discovered, in fact, that a rule is only a rule because exceptions exist (and elite athletes are always the exception) and that the certainties are only valid because, true or false, they work.

I discovered that everything and its opposite can produce the same result by conflicting pathways which are not always explicable.

This, then, is the message contained between the lines of each of the pages of this book. The champions and their coaches have cleared a path to success by means of hard work, reflection, retracing their steps, and with doubt and denial. They have forged a mode of conduct, employing their own not very orthodox or numerous rules. They have evolved a theory from their practice and delivered it to you, incomplete and sometimes contradictory, but so strong in the certainty of their experience, and so true because their winning performances confirm.

There is not only one truth, but many...

BIBLIOGRAPHY

These references were used to complete and to enrich comments held by the interviewees. They constitute a documentary source indispensable for anyone who wants to know more about the triathlon.

BURKE E.-R. – *Serious Cycling.* Human Kinetics, 1995.

BURKE E.-R. – *High-Tech Cycling.* Human Kinetics, 1996.

CAZORLA G., MILLET G. – *Tests spécifiques d'évaluation du triathlète.* FFTRI, 1996.

CHOLLET D. – *Natation sportive, approche scientifique.* Vigot, 1997 (second edition).

COSTILL D.-L., MAGLISCHO E.-W., RICHARDSON A.-B. – *Swimming. Handbook of Sports Medicine and Science.* IOC/FINA, Blackwell Science, 1995.

FLEURANCE P. (coordination) – *Entraînement mental et sport de haute performance.* The Training books of the INSEP N ° 22 , 1998.

GERBEAUX M., BERTHOIN S. – *Aptitude et pratique aérobies chez l'enfant et d'adolescent.* PUF, 1999.

HAUSSWIRTH C. – *Étude des altérations du coût énergétique de la course à pied au cours du triathlon et du marathon.* Thèse, 1996.

HAUSSWIRTH C., LEHÉNAFF D., DRÉANO P., SAVONEN K. – «Effects of Cycling Alone or in a Sheltered Position on Subsequent Running Performance during a Triathlon.» *Med Sci Sports Exerc,* Vol. 31(4): 599-604, 1999.

HÉLAL H. (coordination) – *Sport de haut niveau et récupération.* The Training books of the INSEP n° 27, 2000.

HELLEMANS J. – *Triathlon. A Complete Guide for Training and Racing.* Reed, 1993.

LAVOIE J.-M., MONTPETIT R.-R. – *Applied Physiology of Swimming.* Sports Medicine, 3: 165-199, 1986.

LEHÉNAFF D. – *De la spécificité du triathlon.* An analysis of physiological and technical data collected on triathletes during competition. Diploma of the INSEP, in July, 1993.

LEHÉNAFF D. (coordination) – «Triathlon, Technical and educational file.» *Revue EPS,* n° 259, May-June 1996.

LEHÉNAFF D. (coordination) – *Un sport, deux enchaînements, trois disciplines: le triathlon.* From the 1-st international symposium of training in triathlon. The Training books of the INSEP N ° 20 , 1997.

LEHÉNAFF D. – «Historical, Philosophical, Contextual and Organisational Environments of Modern Sport: Towards a Definition of Quality in Triathlon.» From of the sixth Congress of the European Association of management of triathlon, Madeira, 30 September–4 October 1998.

LEHÉNAFF D. (coordination) – *Triathlon Sydney 2000.* From the second international congress of triathlon of the INSEP. The Training books of the INSEP, n ° 24, 1999

LEHÉNAFF D., BERTRAND D. – *Le Triathlon.* Chiron, 2001 (new edition).

LEHÉNAFF D., HANON C., GAJER B., VOLLMER J.-C., MATHIEU-THÉPAUT C. – «Physiological characterization and comparison of two sessions of track." Seen again(revised) with the AEFA, n ° 155 , 1999.

MATHIEU-THÉPAUT C. (coordination) – *Entraînement de la force. Spécificité et planification.* Les Cahiers de l'INSEP, n° 21, 1997.

NEWBY-FRASER P., MORA J.-M. – *Paula Newby-Fraser's Peak Fitness for Women.* Human Kinetics, 1995.

NOAKES T.-N. – *Lore of Running.* Human Kinetics, 1991.

O'TOOLE M.-L., DOUGLAS P.-S., HILLER W.D.-B. – «Applied Physiology of a Triathlon.» *Sports Medicine,* 8(4): 201-225, 1989.

O'TOOLE M.-L., DOUGLAS P.-S. – « Applied Physiology of Triathlon.» *Sports Medicine,* 19(4): 251-267, 1995.

PRADET M. – *La Préparation physique.* INSEP, 1997.

RICHÉ D. – *L'Alimentation du sportif en 80 questions.* Vigot, 1998.

RICHÉ D. – *Guide nutritionnel des sports d'endurance.* Vigot, 1999 (second edition).

SCOTT D. – *Dave Scott's Triathlon Training.* Fireside, 1986.

SLEAMAKER R., BROWNING R. – *Serious Training for Endurance Athletes.* Human Kinetics, 1996.

SVENSSON T. – *The Total Triathlon almanac 3.* Trimarket, 1996.

WEINECK J. – *Manuel d'entraînement.* Vigot, 1997 (fourth edition).

WERCHOSCHANSKI J.-W. – *L'Entraînement efficace.* 1992.

WILMORE J.-H., COSTILL D.-L. – *Physiology of Sport and Exercise.* Human Kinetics, 1994.